DOROTHEE SOELLE

THE ARMS RACE KILLS

Even Without War

Translated by
GERHARD A. ELSTON

FORTRESS PRESS　　　　PHILADELPHIA

Library of Congress Catalog Card Number 82-48543

ISBN 0-8006-1701-0

9772E83   Printed in the United States of America   1-1701

CONTENTS

TRANSLATOR'S NOTE

These are radio broadcasts, speeches, and articles that were originally directed to a German audience on topics of urgency also for Americans; it is important for us to understand how a significant sector of our Christian community in Germany thinks and feels about such topics. That, of course, compounds the translator's difficulties. I have, therefore, tried to put into footnotes explanations of references to persons, quotations, and events that would be familiar to most Germans, but may not be to many U.S. readers. I ask the indulgence of those who will find these footnotes repetitious of the well known. Some evocations simply cannot be duplicated in a translation: for example, a German church audience would resonate to the last line in the Lenten sermon on envy because it quotes a familiar hymn—no such easy recognition is possible among us. Having experience as an interpreter more than as a translator, I do hope I have managed to capture the mood as well as the meaning on issues that have been central to my life on both continents. Bible quotations are from the Revised Standard Version except for the quotation from the Sermon on the Mount (Matt. 6:26–27 in chapter 4) and from 1 John 3:16 in chapter 5, where the New English Bible more closely reflects Luther's German translation as used by the author.

GAE

1
THE ARMS RACE KILLS EVEN WITHOUT WAR*

The West German rock band *ideal* does a song entitled "Execution," which runs:

> Come to the wall to get gunned down,
> hand in hand we both will fall.
> Come my friend let us get wasted
> with our backs against the wall.

The song ends with the line "today I'm crazy to hear shots." The words "to hear shots" are then repeated more than twenty-five times.

If you expose yourself to this music, you will need no further instruction on the connection between aggression and self-aggression, hate and self-hatred, killing and the killing of oneself, murder and suicide. Ever since the NATO decision of 12 December 1979,[1] the arms race has become not only the central topic of politics, but also a primary cultural event. After all, the preparation of nuclear holocaust and the planning of mass murder and suicide is not merely a concern of the military establishment.

The arms race is not preparation for something that may happen in the future or that may never happen, as we are hopefully and continually assured. Rather, the arms race is a state between peace and war with a clear trend—we prepare

---

*Slightly shortened version of a contribution to *Dialektik. Beiträge zu Philosophie und Wissenschaften* ("Dialectic: Contributions to Philosophy and the Sciences") 4, 1982.

1. The NATO decision to station a new generation of United States intermediate-range missiles (Pershing II and Cruise) in Europe.

for war for so long that it finally strikes us as normal. This is affirmed daily by rhetorical derailments (a winnable nuclear war, an atomic war restricted to Europe, an atomic warning shot) that come to us from the United States and that our government then busily seeks to dampen, to "translate" differently, to "interpret" in context. Daily, a little more poison is injected into the minds and hearts of people, a little more conditioning to death. Thinking the unthinkable must be learned.

> Boredom kills, but much too slowly
> you will find this helps us lots.
> Today I have a vicious feeling
> today I'm crazy to hear shots.

Such texts are strangely ambivalent, at least to older persons observing this culture. Are they intended ironically? For example, "luxury" is noisily touted as the highest value, as if it were a lover. Is this supposed to unmask the addiction to luxury of the dominant class? Concerning the "shots," I am not entirely clear as to who is the subject and who is the object. Is it good and pleasurable to shoot someone, or to be shot? I pose these simplistic questions quite aware that the answers to them will turn out to be something like: Sure. Both. Anything. All the same.

In the New Wave music there is no self that segregates itself from the world in utter world-weariness. Hatred and contempt include the self, and target it aggressively. Whatever it is that fascinates people seems to flow in utter conformity from the highest levels of this society, for example, money and power. That is why the irony is never unambiguous, for that would call for a lucid stance above all this: to assert the individual self or the community in opposition to the world. No critical attitude is rehearsed; despair over luxury and killing does not—yet ?—become revolutionary. What I hear in this music is that the arms race kills—even without war.

You cannot call the condition under which we live "peace." Each day there are fifteen thousand casualties in the war of the rich against the poor.[2] The bombs are falling now, as the American peace movement puts it. This slogan has provided me with a flash of new insight. It has become clearer to me that you do not "prepare" for mass annihilation in the same way that you make provisions for other anticipated events. It is furthermore no longer appropriate to speak of "organized absence of peace."[3] We are already confronted by organized mass destruction when children under two years of age die from starvation at the rate of one every minute.[4] We must finally take note of that *now*. Such preparation characterizes our present. Preparation of nuclear war is the law by which we live; it governs my stroll along the Elbe River just as it conditions the rock band's music.

The assumption that it is possible to plan a future, think about it, work and pay for it, while at the same time want to prevent this future is not a productive contradiction but ordinary self-deception. It is a lie that strikes back and will haunt us. Such technical military terminology as "political weapons" express this lie—as if the technology of mass annihilation could be developed, tested, put into production, used in training; as if you could learn to operate it without real consequences and with "mere political significance." For this technology, the old-fashioned appellation "weapons" is about as appropriate as referring to the Zyclon B gas that was used at Auschwitz as a "weapon."

The dialectic of this age in which we live cannot be quite that simple. [The future that we design and willingly plan changes our present without our will.] The future is the

2. These figures are estimates published by the Food and Agriculture Organization (FAO) in Rome.
3. A widely quoted expression originated by Dieter Senghaas, a leading German peace researcher.
4. Estimate, FAO.

mother of the present—projected but nonetheless real. The threshold of restraint against killing is lowered in anticipation of the future. This creates the present conditions of violence. Military rearmament dictates social disarmament, as in the United States where a pre-Franklin Delano Roosevelt state of living outside the protection or the rule of law is being re-established for the underprivileged. This is clearly evident. But this also destroys other areas of life. What meaning can be attached to schools as an institution if they are subject to entry by military officers?[5] How can you work in a health care system while training for triage in emergency service, learning to divide victims into groups to be aided "now," "not yet," and "not at all"? How can a Cabinet member who professionally calculates and defends levels of megadeaths make a Memorial Day speech honoring the memory of victims of the Second World War?

Every form of preparation for the military use of atomic power destroys those who are "preparing." "I ain't gonna study war no more," says an old pacifist song, and rightly so. To "study war" is more than rehearsal for later or for never. It means becoming accustomed to shooting people, lowering the threshold of restraint, becoming familiar with the possibility of catastrophe. Thinking the unthinkable is no mere game plan for general staff school, it has to become an ever more pervasive educational guideline if mass loyalty is to be maintained.

Atomic weapons development carries with it a totalitarian quality akin to Hitler's "total war." The mass fad "to hear shots" calls for a consensus that must be brought about by ideological national government structures. Deviation, "too much pacifism," must be suppressed at work and at school. Can we regard the desire to kill others as a psychological

5. There has been considerable controversy in West Germany over the rulings that made such intrusion possible.

consequence of the arms race? This kind of consequence is analogous to the side effects of a drug in medicine. It is too bad if the patient has died of what is defined as a mere "side effect," quite apart from what scientific nomenclature designates as the "main" effect. The security which the military preparedness folk are trying to sell us on has a dead certainty about it. A culture dominated by militarism—in its science, its technology, and its economy—will show ever increasing totalitarian tendencies. In Latin America, the political ideology of "national security" allows torture to go unpunished; in our country they can prevent you from practicing your profession, criminalize, and slander you.[6] A postal clerk who is a member of the DKP[7] becomes a "security risk." It is then evident that the millions of people who are committed to peace must also represent a "security risk"—for instance, the more than 2.1 million Germans who, as I write, have signed the Krefeld appeal.[8] If current policies continue, internal repression and the dismantling of democracy are bound to intensify.

The Conservatives are not so far wrong when they insist that one of the chief characteristics of the peace movement is a yearning or longing. To be sure, they hardly know what such a longing is or can accomplish. To denigrate it they attach a "mere" or "simple" to the longing. They thus miss or misun-

6. A West German law allows persons to be excluded from certain civil service professions on the basis of previous associations (even prior to the passage of this legislation), including a number of student organizations which are all quite legal.

7. DKP (German Communist Party)—one of the communist political parties legalized in West Germany some years back in contrast to the outlawed KPD (Communist Party of Germany).

8. Krefeld Appeal—one of several recent German peace manifestoes. This declaration was voted by the one thousand participants in the Krefeld Forum held 15–16 November 1980. It urges the German federal government to withdraw its approval for the stationing of the Pershing II and other new missiles, and in the future to have Germany take an anti-arms race stance within NATO.

derstand the religious dimension which is truly part of the peace movement. They do not understand that human beings are seeking God when they begin to turn into a "resistance movement against death," as Christoph Blumhardt, a nine-teenth-century religious socialist, called Christianity. You can-not seek God while you prepare yourself for mass murder, just in case.

What then happens to peace under the balance of terror? It will be regarded as a business, like any other. It rests on bilateral agreements, arms control arrangements, summit meetings, all following a familiar pattern. Every politician anxiously struggles to retain as many as possible of the lovely killer toys and to fox the other side out of as many as possible. But is that a sufficient philosophy of peace? Until now, the so-called balance has produced only permanent escalation. Arms controls have been counterproductive, because the prohibi-tion of a few weapons allows for the development of others. Evidently peace built on terror is not peace. The common assumption that peace can be achieved by "treaties" involves a kind of naive rationalism—as if covenants and understandings could replace true understanding, as if you could conclude transactions without acting. Is it not possible that some things cannot be bought in a businesslike way?

Let me use a personalized model. A conflict between two partners can perhaps be ameliorated and made more bearable through discussion, contracts, and mutual consideration. But genuine change and a solution are possible only if one of the partners is willing to take a step out of that inflexible situation; if one of them will no longer insist on what is, but musters the strength for a unilateral initiative; if the love of peace of one of the conflicting partners runs deep enough for him or her to actually put weapons aside, to disarm. Conflict is not resolved by reinforcing existing power relationships with threats to apply more power. What is renewing, productive, what opens up fresh options is precisely any step taken by the one who acts without making himself dependent on the other.

The preparation of nuclear holocaust is a crime according to international law and even according to the fundamental constitutional law of the German Federal Republic. The fact or the assumption that others are committing the same crime in no way alters the criminality, any more than do lies that redefine war as defense and rearmament as merely catching up. The challenge is to overcome bilateral thinking. Only those who unilaterally stand up for peace really understand what is at stake. The more lucidly the peace movement articulates its concerns, the more self-evident the idea of unilateral renunciation of violence becomes.

My most important conceptual achievement during the past several years, that is, since 12 December 1979, which I regard as one of the black days in our history, has been to progress from bilateralism to unilateralism. I have learned that my hope for bilateral arms limitation was trivial and lacked seriousness. To hype peace evenhandedly shows but superficial love of peace. True education for peace goes beyond business conferences. The arms race kills, and bilateralism is no more than a business practice.

We must begin unilaterally in order to progress bilaterally. Everything new has a unilateral beginning. That is also true of nuclear pacifism as the moral and political minimum; it cannot be attained by bargaining, calculation, or weighed on a scale. Bilateralism represents the old belligerence and absence of peace as well as the very latest. Some things are existential in the sense that you cannot pursue them with others serving as a reference point. In religious faith, whatever you may know about others and their relation to God is of no interest: it is up to you! Everything existential is necessarily unilateral, and peace is an existential category. I rather think that the mistrust by so many, especially the young, of leading politicians is founded on the fact that these gentlemen are not regarded as

Peace as business vs.
spirituality

capable of peace because they have turned peace into a business. They act like merchants who trade in deterrence. By contrast there is a peace movement spirituality that simply cannot accept precisely this affront to the dead of an earlier day and this crime against today's poor.

The old categories of existentialism emerge again. There is anxiety, there are the dreams of emigration, there are young women who migrate out of their own bodies, never to bear a child into this world! Hence the unavoidable imperative of the political issue of peace, even if it is always tied to other themes, such as antiimperialism and solidarity with the Third World. This is something that we cannot delegate to peace technocrats. It is this depth of personal involvement that drives people out into the street and into the innumerable groups, initiatives, and single-action responses. It is as if people were struggling desperately against being incarcerated in some Orwellian bunker.

In my mind, the slogan "the arms race kills, even without war" has a theological dimension. Perhaps you cannot even understand it without at least some residual faith in God. Belief in a shalom-peace grounded in justice and offering happiness; hope in the future of the human family; unconditional love of all that lives: these are experiences and designs that transcend the given and the visible. That is why tradition refers to faith, hope, and love as the "supernatural virtues." They presuppose that emphatic concept of life with which the Bible operates. Not just any continued vegetating under the balance of terror deserves to be called "life." Nor can you peddle each acquiescence in the capacity of nuclear blackmail as "securing the peace." "The peace of God, which passes all understanding, will keep your hearts and your minds in Christ Jesus" (Phil. 4:7). This peace which is above our calculations is not to be confused with an inner condition of harmony into which an individual may withdraw. What it does mean is peace "in the world but not of this world" which spreads among us and grows as a political force within the movement for peace. But it is not rooted in any level of our capitalist mentality. The arms race kills; it is the peace produced by "this" world. We stand in need of a different peace, because we still need another world.

2

AUSCHWITZ AND NO END IN SIGHT*

I cannot discourse on this topic. I cannot develop and debate the thesis implied by the title, question it, or confirm it. If words do not fail you on certain matters, then you had none in the first place, paraphrasing Lessing's remark about intelligence.[1] The language of discourse and discussion becomes mindless in the face of some events: indeed, it would imply a kind of neutral complicity.

What I shall attempt is to convey what is in my mind through the language of meditation and storytelling. It is a reminding in the double sense of that phrase: I call to mind and preserve the memory, and I greatly mind the implied thesis of the title. I cannot accept it, it had better not be true. For how am I to live if it is truth?

Since discourse is impossible, I shall move from meditation toward something that I find extremely difficult but at least possible. This all but impossible speaking in the face of devastating reality is called "prayer" in our tradition. It is a way to say no to what is a fact.

BEFORE AND AFTER

A year ago, my friend and former colleague Robert McAffee Brown took me to visit Elie Wiesel, the author, himself an

---

*First printed in Karl-Klaus Rabe, ed., *Vier Minuten vor Mitternacht. Stellungnahmen zum Rüstungswahnsinn* ("Four Minutes to Midnight: Positions on the Madness of the Arms Race.") Bornheim-Merten: Lamuv Verlag, 1981.
1. Gotthold Ephraim Lessing (1729–81). German dramatist and critic, advocate of freedom of thought.

Auschwitz survivor, who coined the term "holocaust" lest Hitler's language survive in phrases such as "final solution" or "extermination," and lest the language of neutrality survive in expressions such as "catastrophe" or "genocide." The conversation in Wiesel's apartment overlooking New York's Central Park had two focuses, centers of gravity.

There are plans for a holocaust monument in the United States. Elie Wiesel chairs the commission whose chief difficulty appears to be the limitation or selection of the victims. Was it only Jews who were exterminated like vermin, or also Gypsies and homosexuals as well?

More and more ethnic groups raise their voices and wish to remember their dead and their annihilation—Estonians, Lithuanians, Latvians, Kurds, . . . and others. While we talked the telephone kept ringing, making Wiesel wince—he is a slight, easily perturbed man—as he took up the receiver. The above issue was then critical: how to balance off the dead; a question of competitive suffering; a gruesome, impossible, unavoidable question.

The other focus of our conversation was more personal. Wiesel told us about his relationship with his eight-year-old son. Each evening father and son share an hour, carefully reserved. Wiesel said that because of this he does not like to travel and takes his son along whenever possible. There are some rules for this time together. Each may ask anything. Each will answer to the best of his knowledge. The boy, for instance, may ask his father to talk about his schooldays. What was it like when you were a boy? He asks about the teachers, about schoolmates. The father tells him a great deal. Sometimes the boy will then ask questions such as: Where is your friend now? Or: Is that teacher still alive? What happened then? Does the cherry tree still grow in the uncle's garden? And the father does not answer. He does not speak. He is silent. And one day the boy puts a strange question to his father. He asks: Was it before or after? The father has told the child nothing about deportation or extermination camps, about gas. And yet the boy knows something and translates it into the words "before" and "after." That was before, Dad, right? he says. Some day the father will have to tell him what happened between before and after.

I mention this because I want to sharpen our consciousness of that time. There is a "before" and there is an "after." The child now growing up in Manhattan will one day have to fill the gap between "before" and "after" with knowledge, with dates and information. And we too, living "after," should know what occurred. The phrase "no end in sight" does not mean to imply that it was ever so, since Cain slew Abel, and that it shall continue always. Whatever we forget or suppress we are doomed to repeat—as victims? as prison guards? as spectators? I shall have to leave that question unanswered. But I do believe that every member of our society, even the younger ones, should be expected to live "after" and to know what that means.

STAR, SMOKE, HAIR

The central event in this century's German history dare not be forgotten or relegated to secondary status within our total cultural context. I want to cite some experiences which affected me both personally and in my national identity.

When, in 1946, I had a chance to listen to Bach's *St. Matthew Passion* again, for the first time after the Nazi period, the powerful chorus "His blood be on us and on our children" was omitted. What had passed "before" had become impossible "after." The event has sullied words, language, thoughts, and images and given them a different meaning. This impossibility to speak "after" as one did "before," as if nothing had happened, radically affects the relationship of a writer to the language. As an author I need a self-conscious sense of language; I cannot ignore history or that event. Words have lost their original innocence. When I think of innocent words such as star, or hair, or smoke, then as a writer I am obliged to know the resonance that comes with these words. What associations do they conjure up? What is the difference when they are used in 1930 or 1943 or 1980? Can anyone who writes in German and is linguistically aware and sensitive use a word such as star as if it simply referred to a heavenly body? Suppose I realize that I am living "after," suppose I wish to remember, can I then ever hear the word star without thinking of those yellow stars?[2] Is smoke still a symbol of peace, of the village, of home, as with Hoelderlin, so long "before"?[3] Is hair still merely hair? Paul Celan understood this and demands that linguistically we live "after" and not "before."[4] We learn to listen to his language and to endure it. But how much more poorly do we cope with such ideological words as obedience, duty, national loyalty, patriotism, etc. They still carry their historical baggage. Auschwitz and no end in sight!

THE OBSOLESCENCE OF EXPERIENCE

But can you actually burden people with this way of enduring the "after"? What is the younger generation to do with it? Are we to rewrite our encyclopedias, change our history books, censure our jokes? It is impossible to salvage certain implications across generations. Nothing brings my own aging home to me as clearly as the impossibility of passing on to my children the meaning of Auschwitz for my generation. Of course I try. Of course I find it monstrous that people who can explain quantum theory are unfamiliar with the words selec-

2. Yellow stars of David which Jews were ordered to wear sewn to their clothing.
3. J. C. Friedrich Hoelderlin (1770–1843). German lyric, neo-Hellenist poet who linked the classic and romantic schools.
4. Paul Celan, pseudonym of Paul Antschel (1920–70). Rumanian-born, eventually French citizen, regarded by many critics as the most significant German language poet in the post-World War II period. Some of his poetry deals with the Nazi death camps and relations of Germans and Jews. "Death Fugue" and many of his other poems have been translated.

tion, ramp, Zyclon B. Of course I keep asking myself how we might transmit the history of shame. And yet I sense the gulf of the generation gap. If I and others of my generation spent ten years of our lives wondering "how could this happen?" then I cannot, for instance, condense this inquiry, its methods, and any partial results into a four-unit curriculum. It is not simply a question of information. I find the greatest obstacle in the difficulty of transmitting emotions after such a long time. How can I preserve feelings of shame and guilt so that they will not be forgotten? How can we create a national identity that will not "rework" this past of ours, but pass it on?

True, I struggle against my own aging, against the fact that my experience is turned into discardable experience. But I also struggle against anyone proclaiming in my country that "we have made it again," which I hear clearly as a repudiation of the feeling of collective guilt and shame. Our public historical forgetfulness is monstrous. We have turned a veterans' Memorial Day into a Day of Public Mourning, but there is no day to remember the Jewish victims; we have relatively decent television programs—by international standards—but the holocaust film, an attempt to educate a broad spectrum of people about that event, was not produced by people in charge in this country. Other films, such as the German Democratic Republic's (East Germany) unforgettable *Jacob the Liar* barely made the program.[5]

If we had truly made a new beginning in Germany after 1945, it would surely be reflected in institutions that allow some measure of recollection: in the naming of universities, schools, and streets, in holidays and their rituals, in the way research questions and queries are posed by the sciences. Our awareness of the "before" and "after" might be expressed in

5. *Jacob der Luegner* ("Jacob the Liar") by Jurek Becker, one of only a few GDR-produced films (1975) to be shown in the United States, is set in a Polish ghetto during the Nazi occupation. It was nominated for an academy award as best foreign film.

the manner in which we handle our cultural heritage and, as a moral minimum, in our respect for the dead. Perhaps the most important assertion we can make about God nowadays is that he is the memory that forgets no one. "God is memory," as process theologians have put it. This thesis is a measure of our godlessness: We push God aside because we would rather not be reminded.

WHAT ABOUT GOD?

Before and after—that should have been branded into our culture—especially into our religious culture. But precisely in the churches there has been too little genuine reflection and new thinking. At the 1965 Cologne *Kirchentag*[6] I said something that produced debates, readers' letters, and any amount of public and private controversy, in other words, a great deal of trouble. What I said was: "And since Auschwitz I also do not know how one can praise a God 'who o'er all things so wondrously reigneth.'"[7] That was my way of attempting at least an initial formulation of the theological problem. Can we talk about God "after" precisely as "before"? Is "reigning" an activity of God? Such a God should surely be accused at Nuremberg and condemned as a war criminal![8] A God who has power to intervene but who remains neutrally aloof would deserve our contempt. For one of my generation's fundamental insights is precisely the fact that there is no possible neutrality, no "I really didn't know" in the face of the murder

6. *Kirchentag*—"church day"—the once annual, now biennial mass rallies of the German Protestant churches. *Kirchentage,* and similar meetings of Roman Catholics, are one continuing manifestation of the postwar Christian lay movements in Germany.

7. From the second verse of that most popular hymn, "Praise to the Lord," by Joachim Neander (1630–80), translated by Catherine Winkworth (1829–78).

8. Nuremberg war crimes trials, in which an Allied War Crimes Tribunal tried and convicted top Nazi leaders of war crimes committed in preparation for and during World War II.

of twelve million innocents![9] Does not the burden of history force us to alter our ways of speaking about God, making impossible all superficial theism, the easy assumption of a heavenly Superbeing who knows everything, is everywhere, and has all the power?! At least the three traditional determinants of God as all-knowing, omni-present, and all-powerful (*omniscientia, omnipresentia, omnipotentia*) should be blown away because they cannot be reconciled with lovingkindness, mercy, and compassion. In this way we may properly note the death of this particular god and are made to search for new ways to speak of God. For what can we possibly say about God—"after"? We can say that he is present among those who suffer and is not one of the executioners, is not among the spectators, that he was gassed, that no one could help him because we did not help him, that we should speak of his suffering and not about his power, that he is with the victims of violence rather than with those who practice violence.

The conceptualization of God as the manager of history hides a good dose of fatalism or belief in destiny. It was but the will of God, we say; had God not willed it, it would not have happened. But that is a childish, cult-of-leadership kind of theology. Auschwitz was not the will of God or something that he allowed. It was not done in his name, but in the name of the German people. I rather suspect that fatalism, even if pious, precludes all solidarity. The God of the Bible is a God of ever-subjugated human solidarity which the Scripture refers to as the strength of the weak. He is not the remote, autonomous Lord who has his own inscrutable plans for us. He pulls us unto himself as strongly or as weakly as love will pull—without any coercion. In this vortex of love some did

9. German records indicate that approximately six million Jews and approximately six million other Europeans of diverse backgrounds were put to death in Nazi concentration and extermination camps. These figures are thought to include German political victims, but not the victims of euthanasia of the handicapped or "genetically tainted."

reach a point where they no longer needed to ask: "Why does God permit this?" Whatever happened could not shake their trust in God. Some Jews went praying into the gas chambers; but the God to whom they prayed is not the objectified arbiter of history.

I cannot deal here with all the consequences that the event has for our understanding of God. But I should like to point out one which has only in recent years become apparent to me: the feminist one. I can no longer speak of God in the macho categories of patriarchy, of the doer, the guide, the king, chief, or boss. There are no reasons to love or honor those. We must begin to speak about God with greater precision, in order that our talk about God will illuminate the meaning of our life instead of outlining its domination.

IT IS NOT FINISHED

A second theological rectification is necessitated by life "after"; it concerns the doctrine of Christ. Again, the issue was raised for me by a single sentence. In Cologne we had convened a political Lenten vigil with the theme "It is not finished," and the turmoil caused by this mere title remains unforgettable. In dogmatics you can find a certain christological perfectionism that relates all things to Christ and solves all things in him. Because he has done everything for us, we need not do anything. Because he is salvation, we need no longer wait for the Messiah and, worse, we must persecute those who for two thousand years have not recognized Jesus Christ as the Messiah only because the world did not change, because swords and medium-range missiles have not yet been turned into plowshares and rural health clinics. If you freeze Jesus' saying "it is finished" into rigid ideology, it spawns Christian anti-Judaism with all its gruesome consequences.

We must therefore revise not only our understanding of God, employing a less imperialistic terminology about God, but also our Christology. Jesus was a Jewish proletarian, not a Roman citizen. He hails from below, not above. He lives unprotected and rejects the protection of power. If you distill out of this poor man from Nazareth a Heavenly Being with all might and authority, in whose name women were persecuted and burned as witches and Jews as Christ-killers, this will be in part because of an all too elevated, rarified Christology—a doctrine of Christ that deifies him at the cost of his humanity, that plays down his roots in Judaism and turns him into a redeemer whose divine name we merely need to parrot. But if, on the contrary, we recognize him as our suffering brother and our abused sister, as the very least whom we encounter day by day, then we are within reach of a Christology out of the depth.

A Christ without the Hebrew Bible, without the so-called Old Testament, is no longer a Christ who suffers under injustice but who is triumphant with the rulers. In the United States these days, you can find a religious television culture, the so-called electronic church, which peddles a sentimental, individualistic, successful Jesus. This Jesus is not concerned with hunger, racism, or militarism. He concentrates on the salvation of your very personal soul. He is tailored to middle-class hopes. He has nothing to say to the poor, to single mothers, to young blacks who must chose between prison and the military. Out of his mouth you hear much about salvation and nothing about justice; his Jewishness has been taken away from him. I believe that wherever that occurs nowadays we confront a phenomenon which I am inclined to call Christofascism. Here the authentic, the Jewish, the poor Jesus is forgotten and mollified.

IT CONTINUES

I remember the day my childhood ended, and that day has to do with Auschwitz. In the autumn of 1944 the mother of a half-Jewish classmate came into our home and was hidden there. It was during the period when the hitherto privileged mixed marriages between Jews and "Aryans" were targeted.[10] Those not prepared to divorce had to expect deportation.[11] Jochen Klepper was one who committed suicide together with his wife and daughter because of these measures.[12] This Mrs. B. lived in an attic in our house and was locked in when the cleaning lady came. During air raid alarms at night, when we all moved to a somewhat improved air raid shelter, we could not, of course, take her along. We were always afraid that we would find her wounded under the rubble and we would not be able to call a physician. I talked with her frequently. One day she said to me, "You need not be afraid for me. They won't get me." Then she took a glass bottle out of her pocketbook and placed it in my hand. "That is quite enough poison," she said. That is when I ceased being a child. Suddenly I knew the meaning of the names Buchenwald, Mauthausen, Ravensbrueck; we had not heard of Auschwitz.

On a streetcar I once gazed for a long time at a pale girl with large dark eyes. It was one of those encounters between two people which might lead to anything or nothing at all. I was too shy to speak to her. A fleeting smile touched her face. She clutched a briefcase close to her chest, but when she stepped off I saw the yellow star and could read the letters "Jew." I cannot shake off this image; it was a rainy November evening

10. An "Aryan" was defined by Nazi legislation (all of this, including the concentration camps, was made quite "legal") as someone who could prove that all four grandparents had been "Aryans"—meaning Caucasian, essentially non-Jewish and non-Romany (Gypsy). Restrictions governing those who were part "Aryan" were changed at various times, as were those dealing with "nonAryans" related to "Aryans." Since all this was based on race theories, religious affiliation played no role unless you were converted to Judaism. There were a considerable number of "nonAryan Christians." Like Jesus and the apostles, many of them were one hundred percent Jewish.

11. Deportation was to alleged "labor camps"—several of these did employ forced labor battalions even while functioning as extermination factories.

12. Jochen Klepper (1903–43). German novelist (*The Father*, 1937) and poet, particularly well known for his hymns.

in Cologne. For a moment I thought I would get off too and run after her, but I was too cowardly. Many years later I was reminded of that girl. I saw photographs of children in Vietnam who were being "evacuated" from the so-called free fire zones and, if they were lucky, ended up behind barbed wire. Evacuation was just a word; frequently they were simply "wasted," as a precaution. The American soldiers were given extra Rest and Recreation leave and other privileges if the body count was high. That is what the number of Vietcong killed was called. Only these dead "Vietcong" were not necessarily actual combatants, but Vietnamese women and children and rice farmers. For a long time I did not know what to say. At first I would not believe that our allies, our liberators, the Americans, would plan and carry out programs which were total annihilation sweeps. I felt as did so many good Germans during the Nazi period: "The *Führer* does not know about this!" But the Pentagon knew; the *Pentagon Papers* proved that. And one day I realized that Auschwitz had not ended with Auschwitz. That was the most bitter experience of my adult life.

THE NUCLEAR HOLOCAUST

What conclusions do we draw from this Auschwitz with no end in sight? Since December 1979 NATO has been preparing atomic warfare under American pressure, to which our government submits. I am putting it this way, because the word "defense" when applied to the planned nuclear first strike is devoid of meaning. What is currently projected in the way of military technology and strategy is the preparation of a nuclear holocaust. During the past year I have worked intensively on defense issues, but I do not want to examine all the aspects and details at this time. But if I am to speak seriously—and for me that means theologically—about Auschwitz and no end in sight, then I have to deal with the propaganda to which we are all subjected and which has become a reality in our heads. The arms buildup has been labeled "catching-up," the preparation for a first strike is known as "defense," and the commitment to a total, that is nuclear, arms race is dubbed "modernization." To speak out against this propaganda machine calls for courage and precision, but the knowledge that God is memory will help us, I believe.

I regard what is happening in our country as criminal. Under the Law of Nations, the preparation for an aggressive war is a crime. I perceive this in three different perspectives:

1. Our rearmament provides us with a first-strike capability. It will take us only four minutes to turn the European part of the Soviet Union into a landscape of ruins and corpses.

2. For the Russians, this new threat is the equivalent of a threat to the United States by atomic missiles based in Cuba. In such a case, what would the Americans do if tensions rose even slightly? They would finish off Cuba as a precautionary measure. In precisely that situation the Russians will feel compelled, as a precaution, to finish off Western Europe. We have become the first atomic target.

3. Besides the East-West conflict, there is also the North-South conflict. There is a Third World, and I ask myself whether we are not turning it into an extermination camp. Each bomb that we station here in the name of preparedness hits the poor. The bombs are falling now, as the American peace movement puts it. The nuclear arms race is a crime against the poor. According to Christian doctrine, the earth and all that is in it is the Lord's. In interpreting this biblical saying, the church fathers insisted that everything not essential to one's own needs should be given to the poor. In the light of this tradition, the atomic arms race is the greatest imaginable theft from the poor.

Auschwitz did not end in Auschwitz. What are we to do? Jewish tradition teaches that we must pray and do justice. To do justice in our situation means to participate actively in the peace movement. No one can get away with allegedly not having known. It means not to be compliant but to resist. It means to give bread instead of atomic bombs to the hungry.

To pray means not to despair. We must understand that we are in the midst of the despairing who have already given their consent to death. To pray is to speak out against death.

To pray means to collect ourselves, to reflect, to gain clarity about our direction in life, about our goals for living. It means to remember and in that to achieve a likeness with God, to envision what we seek for ourselves and for our children, to give voice to that vision loudly and softly, together and alone, and thus to become more and more the people we were intended to be.

3

CONSOLATION AND TRUTH:
THE GIFTS OF THE SPIRIT*

When I was a child I never quite knew what to do with a festival such as Pentecost, which had no Christmas tree or Easter bunny. The older I become, the greater is my need to feel something of the blowing of the Spirit. In a nonspiritual age the yearning grows for a Spirit who can give life.[1]

I say this not from a background of an idealistic philosophy of the higher juxtaposed to the low. My background is biblical and realistic. The Hebrew word for spirit is *ruach*, breath, but not just the breath of life with which God blows upon Adam. It also means the wind as a force that can push and drive human beings, overcome them and carry them off, that may ambush or fall upon them and inspire them to words or deeds that far surpass their ordinary capacities. When Rosa Parks remained seated one evening in space reserved for whites only on that bus in Alabama, and that turned into the bus strike organized by Martin Luther King and into a movement and a few more rights for blacks—that was one of those moments of the Spirit. All the stories that we can tell about the Holy Spirit have these two qualities: spontaneity, the unexpected assault, the new that is manifest; and concrete realization, that is, a con-

---

*A Pentecost program of Germany's Southwest Radio in Baden-Baden, broadcast 7 June 1981 as part of a series *Blick in die Zeit* ("Looking at Our Age").

1. The original *geistlos* carries with it several nuances of meaning. Literally, it means "spiritless," but also "mindless" or "lacking any spark." While "nonspiritual" and "without the spirit" seemed appropriate translations for this chapter, the reader may want to keep these multiple meanings in mind.

nection with a particular place and time and a specific situation, not a generality. No one owns the wind, and the Spirit blows where it wills. The early Christians had a classic Greek word for spirit available to them, *nus*, which means timeless truth embodied in the symbol of unchangeable light. They ignored this seemingly suitable term and instead picked a much more unpretentious word to express the new content, namely *pneuma*, which originally meant little more than breath, puff, or wind, but was soon understood as life-giving, animating breath. In neo-Platonic thought, *nus* signified the highest and spiritual level in a human, who was perceived as tripartite: body, soul, and spirit. The Christians chose a word which in pre-Christian Greek implied the subconscious or half-conscious at most. And then they must have shocked many by calling this sensuous, passionate animator spirit holy, of all things—and that brings me back to my opening point, that I greatly miss the Spirit in a nonspiritual age.

If we follow John's Gospel, the Spirit performs two tasks. It consoles and it leads to truth. Both are intimately connected. We go astray if we separate consolation and truth and allow religion to console but forbid it to partake in truth. If the church confines herself to consoling the wretched of this earth and no longer regards even herself as capable of truth, then she will be offering but shallow comfort, limited to the individual person and deferred to the beyond. Then the Sermon on the Mount is turned into a private affair not connected with politics, and the comfort of the Holy Spirit becomes a sentimental substitute for a wasted life. Such comfort cannot fulfill what it promises. The Spirit will console only by illuminating truth, not by abandoning it.

People are quite able to bear truth. That sounds simple, yet it is denied daily by the government and the media. We are told that we are too uninformed and not sufficiently expert to understand the truth. As a woman I am told with particular frequency that I do not, after all, understand anything about atomic energy plants and nuclear weapons, and even more often this is quietly implied. Our country's whole peace movement is charged with naiveté, wide-eyed innocence, one-sidedness, and gullibility. It is as if we were all disqualified from the search for truth, from recognizing truth, and from the fortitude to live truth, and as if the most important decisions about our life and death were appropriately placed in the hands of a few people in Brussels, the headquarters of NATO, and in Washington, the center of the arms race. It is as if we, allegedly the ones in need of protection, were totally incapable of knowing how we might be protected—as if there were no available knowledge about measures that might well end the deadly spiral of the arms race. In such assertions I hear despair about people's capacity for truth, a skepticism that denies the Spirit of God, who comes to us.

Martin Luther said of the Holy Spirit that it was *non scepticus,* not a skeptic. In the New Testament, it is the sophisticated Roman Proconsul Pilate who represents this despairing position with his tired response "What is truth!" to Jesus' claim to be of the truth. He, too, regarded truth as unknowable, least of all by the masses, as too exacting, non-realizable—just as true peace has become merely an illusion to the majority of a population incapable of truth and in this sense bereft of the Spirit.

The Holy Spirit is, at any rate, no skeptic, for it whets our hunger for truth. It inspires in us what Hegel once called the "audacity to insist on truth."[2] It does indeed take courage to demand the truth about the atom bombs scheduled for our country. It takes courage to acknowledge truth, to appropriate all the information provided by neutral peace researchers and to disseminate the truth. A church which may still manage hope for solace but not the courage to demand truth is a church without the Spirit. The Spirit comforted Jesus' disci-

2. G. W. Friedrich Hegel (1770–1831). German philosopher.

ples not merely with the restrictive, protective "Fear Not!" chosen as the theme of the 1981 *Kirchentag*.[3] The Spirit of Pentecost went a bit further in the direction of that other theme that was under discussion for the *Kirchentag* but voted down: "Blessed are the peacemakers!" In this beatitude, consolation and truth are not separated one from the other.

The story that is told to us on the occasion of Pentecost tells of a mighty, tumultuous storm that fills the house, fire rains from the heavens, and a few hitherto quite despondent fishermen begin to preach in public and in a manner that allows them to be understood simultaneously in many languages. The tempest and the fire that fall from the sky serve a new universal language that lifts the old Babylonian confusion of tongues. I believe that the language which is understood today, the fire that burns in the hearts of ever more people, the Spirit that gives courage to demand the truth can be summed up in one word that we had better not abandon to the Spirit-less skepticism of those who are cranking up the arms race spiral of death: Peace!

3. See n. 6, p. 16.

4

ENVY—A DEADLY SIN
AGAINST THE HUMANE*

When Snow White's stepmother is told by the little mirror on the wall that her daughter is many thousand times more beautiful, she turns green with envy and resolves to kill the girl. In Schiller's play *The Outlaws*, Franz Moor compares himself with his more gifted, more amiable, more handsome brother. Envy is his deepest emotion and turns him into a cunning villain.[1]

What is envy? The word reflects a spectrum of meanings: beginning with simply reviewing what is another's, or what he can do or represents, via begrudging it, to hatred, jealousy, compulsive vandalism, resentment, and malicious joy. No one is free of such feelings as "I-should-love-to-have-this" or "I-should-love-to-be-able-to-do-that." Such comparisons are natural and part of our social existence. The Old High German word *Neid* (envy) also meant exertion or competition.[2] Envy is negative only from the point at which a hostile, malevolent feeling becomes part of the comparison. Because others have possessions, traits, abilities, or social status we lack, we envy them. This negativism can go so far that given certain circumstances we would rather see them lose what they have than

---

*First published in Rudolf Walter, *Literarische Fastenpredigten über die Laster in unserer Zeit* ("Literary Lenten Sermons on the Deadly Sins in Our Day") Freiburg-Heidelberg: F. H. Kerle, 1981.

1. Franz Moor is the villain of *Die Räuber* ("The Robbers" or "The Outlaws"), the first of the classic five-act dramas by the German poet and playwright J. C. Friedrich von Schiller (1759–1805).

2. Old High German refers to the language developing in the Southern region of German-speaking lands in the period from about A.D. 750 to the end of the eleventh century.

29

gain it also for ourselves. The aggression against another becomes more important than our own striving for possession.
While we are envious we see ourselves as disadvantaged or
treated unjustly. But instead of joining the struggle for social
justice in concert with others, we allow ourselves to be swal-
lowed up by resentment and become incapable of joy. The
great socialist movements and their leaders did not base their
appeal on envy. There is a song of the American labor movement that goes: "I don't want your millions, mister, I don't
want your diamond ring. . . ." Contempt for those who need
luxury for self-confirmation appeared far more appropriate. To
denigrate the fight for social justice with the catchword "envy"
is unabashed propaganda from above in the class struggle.

In theological tradition, envy has been included among the
seven deadly or mortal sins since the fourth century. It is thus
assumed that envy can destroy our whole connection with life
or our relation to God.

Whatever is that, a mortal sin? According to Roman Catholic teaching, it is a transgression against the ultimate purpose
of the Law, against the love of God, one that is intentional and
serious and therefore leads to eternal damnation unless abso-
lution is granted. "Damnation" sounds strange and not cred-
itable to our ears; but I think we can well understand the
intention when this term is applied to eternity if we just think
of the terrors of impending catastrophe in our era. When air
can no longer be breathed, when water can no longer be
drunk, when hunger cannot be conquered, when you cannot
discount war over ever scarcer resources, then our condition
is not all that far removed from that old traditional image of
hell.

Mortal sins against humaneness nowadays are mortal sins
against humanity. The whole human family is threatened by
the vices of rapacity and greed, by conspicuous waste, and
envy. The militarism that we indulge, the hunger from which
we profit, and the destruction of nature endanger all life on

the planet. Do traditional categories such as mortal sin, vice, and forsaking the Creator to venerate a dead idol still appropriately describe our situation among the death-dealing systems? I believe so, because I am confident that Judeo-Christian tradition can help us reflect, to comprehend what is happening, and to venture change—that is, it may guide us to have faith, to hope, and to love.

What does this tradition offer, critically? It speaks of vices, mortal sins against humaneness, not as particular single transgressions but as habitual practices that constantly spawn acts of like character. Habitual means that a certain stance has become second nature. Vice is achieved by constant repetition, just as is virtue, which can also become habitual. Evil is not a matter of nuclear accidents or isolated catastrophes such as the Three Mile Island nuclear accident.[3] It is the system in which we are at home, to which we have become accustomed, and which will bring about other Three Mile Islands.

This habitual or customary nature of deadly sin is significant because it is relevant in the societal context where certain behavior is desired and supported, praised and rewarded, while other behavior is discriminated against, discouraged, and penalized. It is not individual persons who can determine the societal context of their habitat, what it is to which they must be "habituated," what their "habitual" attitude is to be.

This once again brings me to the topic of reflection about envy. The Old High German word for envy implied, as already stated, exertion and contest. This provides us with the social framework within which envy becomes habitual and a deadly sin: without envy there would be no constant comparison with others; without envy no social climbing; without envy no super feats; without envy no competition. A competitive society is a society of envy.

3. The reference is to the accident at the Three Mile Island nuclear power station near Harrisburg, Pennsylvania, in March 1979.

The traditional concept of sin is incomprehensible if you interpret it simply individualistically. Envy does not grow solely out of my genetic predisposition, my psychic inheritance, my family situation—for example, the fact of growing up as the middle child of three. Envy is also conditioned by the world into which we grow, by the expectations directed at us. Perhaps my world has always assumed that I will stare jealously at another's possessions or ability, that I would screech "gimme!" as soon as I learned to talk. Perhaps the production of all those unnecessary goods has been in collusion with my instincts of envy, and appeals to them in advertising, induces them in education, and rewards them on the social escalator.

At any rate, sin is more than individual failure. Sin and social context belong together. That is why the Hebrew Bible constantly speaks of the transgression of the people, identifying it as a turning from God and the worship of idols. Mortal sin, namely, sin that leads to death and orients us toward death, is both social compulsion and personal guilt at one and the same time. We are all subject to sinful coercion. Competitive thinking is practiced in every classroom; the grading system objectifies inequality, making it universally accessible and significant, so that finally inequality is viewed as a natural circumstance. Consumerism is washed into our brains by radio and television programs. The notion that by having more we shall be more is implicit in an economy geared to continuous growth.

This system leads us into sin. It has power over individuals who cannot do or leave undone what they chose, as if we were free agents. I must practice consumerism and purchase superfluous things lest my little nine-year-old daughter become envious. The envy that school children express with their "but mom, everybody wears one!" is part of the system that governs my life. The New Testament, especially St. Paul, uses images when speaking about sin which illustrate this power of sin that is integral to a system and beyond the individual. It commands hosts to subjugate other lands, it keeps slaves, coercing humans, binding them, selling them, incarcerating them, deceiving them so that they will know no world other than that of sin. It flaunts its sway: we are to regard this world of avarice and greed, of envy and possessiveness, as normal.

I mention this biblical finding firstly to forestall the common individualistic misunderstanding that it is purely each individual's attitude that determines our sinfulness; and, secondly, I wish to repudiate the post-Christian popular-psychology misunderstanding that since all matters concerning me were determined during my prenatal and early infancy phases, we can no longer speak of sin except as though every personal failing were fully explained by a reference to an authoritarian father or an overprotective mother. This kind of pop psychology actually reinforces the prison walls of sin in certain ways. If we follow biblical tradition and recognize as sin all those forces that seek to seduce us to ill will and hatred, to fear, and to unhappiness over the good fortune of others, instead of accepting them as the psychic fate of any individual within the achievers' society, then we are taking up the battle against these powers. If we can speak of sin we have already left its dominion; such talk implies critical awareness. That is, when we cease to goose step along in the mighty army of sin, we cease to grant it power over us and no longer deny the might of Christian liberty. We are neither born nor condemned to envy.

Whether envy is a basic anthropological category of human behavior, or whether it may be overcome, is still being hotly debated. The first view believes that society must develop a system of social controls and institutionalize the avoidance of envy, as happens in sports that have not yet been commercialized. From the second perspective, it is not merely a matter of rules to minimize envy, but of creating such social conditions of equality as would make life without envy possible. Of course the two approaches are not mutually exclusive. If in some countries children wear a school uniform, this regulation averts envy, but it also establishes a measure of equality. If the filthiest and dreariest jobs in a society draw higher compensation than more congenial or intelligent work, that too reduces envy. Thus revives the old dream of life unencumbered by possessions, masters, or envy, where all things are available to all to use. "Look at the birds of the air: they do not sow and reap and store in barns," they do not own, they do not envy, we might continue, "yet your heavenly Father feeds them. You are worth more than the birds! Is there a man of you who by anxious thought can add a foot to his height?" (Matt. 6:26–27). There is a tendency in the Gospels toward freedom from property, violence, rulers; in short, an anarchic trend that goes beyond the shunning of envy. Once, when the disciples, anxiously concerned about hierarchical protocol and full of envy, seek to send away mothers who are approaching Jesus with their children, he says: "Let the children come to me, and do not hinder them; for to such belongs the kingdom of God. Truly, I say to you, whoever does not receive the kingdom of God like a child shall not enter it" (Luke 18:16–17). Rank, wealth, privilege, and prestige are abolished and thereby envy is made impotent. It is the Christian view that it is possible to overcome that deadly sin envy, it is possible to free yourself from a society that forces you to sin. If the objective conditions of inequality and privilege that create envy are changed, then envy will no longer be glorified as a principle of life. It becomes once again what it was in the first place: sin—the sin of loving death more than life, of seeking and valuing what is dead rather than pursuing what is alive.

Once we understand the constraints created by a society built on competitiveness, we shall begin to oppose them. The opposite of sin as a habit is not merely moral virtue, but faith that a different kind of life is attainable. Faith demands clarity and a warrior's determination, a kind of valor. Envy will dim and wreck such valor, because in envy we turn back upon ourselves, shackle ourselves to our old self. Luther described a sinner as a person twisted back upon himself (*homo incurvatus in seipsum*). Envy illustrates that. Those possessed by it can see nothing but themselves. Their lives' point of view will not allow even the possibility of selfless joy. Everything is examined in the perspective of self-aggrandizement. Like a tourist who invades a country to pick up as souvenirs whatever treasures of nature and of art, of the other people's culture, can be found, just so the envier is blind to everything that cannot be photographed, taped, filmed, or purchased. "The place was dead" in tourist language usually means "There was nothing to buy." Because of this extreme and rigid egoism, envy also wrecks all aesthetic feeling. Those who are driven by envy cannot surrender to anything other or alien, however beautiful and self-contained. They can love beauty only by owning it or seeking to obtain it.

Perhaps this joylessness, this incapacity for pleasure, is another traditional characteristic of envy. Thomas Aquinas associates envy with sadness, with *tristitia*. In his thought, envy violates not justice, but love. He defines it as grief over your neighbor's affluence, and concludes that it will contribute to your misfortune and effect a reduction in your own wealth. This definition is of interest. Thomas assumes that your neighbor's prosperity may bring you joy or distress. I can react with either envy or gladness when another is blessed with goods or competence which I lack. I can view another's greater wealth as an impairment of my own estate, or I can be pleased by his good fortune and be the stronger for it myself. Another's fortune can be my delight or it can diminish me, shame me, and hence give me grief. Thus envy becomes the antithesis of love. Love takes pleasure in another's achievements, but envy is distressed thereby, and will feel burdened. Inasmuch as envy counters love it is a vice, a mortal sin.

What we can learn from Thomas is that people are in really
sad shape if their neighbor's good fortune leads not to felicita-
tion and vicarious rejoicing but to depression. Other human
beings are perceived not as a rich blessing but as peril. This
prevents even the possibility of good will without ulterior
motive, or any innocent satisfaction about another person who
has something I do not have or is capable of doing what I
cannot. Unhappiness isolates, or should we say: isolation
makes us miserable. What is important, at any rate, is to note
the joylessness, the torture, inherent in envy. Envy gnaws, it
is wormwood to us, as the saying goes.

If I look into my own conscience and think about what
makes me envious, the first thing that comes to mind is the
attitude of the older generation, of which I am a part, toward
the younger. How much better off they are than I was! They
do not know hunger, they do not know privation, they are not
subject to the kind of repression I still had to face. Sexual envy
of people who are having a much easier time of it is surely a
major part of it, as is envy of the idlers who do not have to
work nearly so hard, and envy of their vacation and leisure
culture which offers them so many more choices. There is
distress hidden in this my envy, fear of having been short-
changed, jealousy and, occasionally, when something does not
quite work out for these younger folk, malicious glee. How
can I learn to let go of this envy, so typical of my generation?
The first step is awareness. Envy is so ugly that we have a hard
time recognizing it in ourselves, let alone admitting to it. It is
easier to conceal it from myself. The more conscious I am of
my own feelings, the more I am in touch with myself and hold
myself accountable, the more sensitive I shall be toward
others. Instead of envying them blindly, I come to know their
problems and difficulties and am able to correct my silly
prejudice that tells me "do they ever have it made."

There is yet another path in my self-education against envy.
That has to do with my effort to turn distress over someone

else's good fortune to empathetic gladness. I have a natural tendency to take my misery seriously, to value it highly. I am not feeling well today, I say, and frequently that means that I refuse to deal with my wretchedness. I shall therefore not discover that my pain or my often indeterminate melancholy is based on the nasty calamity of another's good luck and is rooted in a grudge against life. If I begin with a critical assessment of my misery, then I shall learn to understand that envy is a theological dilemma, a sin which separates me from that great life we call God, isolates, and demolishes me. I shall then discover that my woe is nothing profound or even special, and I shall wish to break out of that prison. This process which I have just referred to as "discovering" and "wishing," we might just as well call "praying." It is an attempt at colloquy, the Great Dialogue,—something like this:

Free me from the desolation that holds me prisoner.
Restore to me the joy of that other life.
Let me praise all that is younger and more beautiful, richer and stronger.
Fire of love, you can melt away the envy within me.
Wind of the spirit, you can make me hear.
Sun of righteousness, shine upon us.

5

LIFE AS A RETURNING*

Dear sisters and brothers, we are a letter from Christ. St. Paul applies this term to the congregation at Corinth. He tells them that they are a letter from Christ, "written not with ink but with the Spirit of the living God, not on tablets of stone but on tablets of human hearts" (2 Cor. 3:3). At the same time Paul mentions that this letter from Christ is "to be known and read by all."

How to be a Christian is something you do not learn from books or information packets, but primarily from other human beings. I want to tell you about a person who has become such a letter from Christ to me: a woman, an American, a Catholic nun. She is one of the four women who were murdered in El Salvador early in December 1980.[1] Ita Ford was a Maryknoll sister, a member of the missionary order of women who do not reside in convents but in slums together with the poor for whom they live. They do not wear religious habits, but civilian garb. I have seen snapshots of Ita Ford and I should have taken her for a bank employee or perhaps a teacher; quite an ordinary woman, forty years old, likable, not especially good-looking, inspiring confidence. This woman has become a letter from Christ to me. She represents something of that "living credibly" which we all seek.

Ita Ford was born in Brooklyn in 1940. After college, at age

---

*Address given 20 June 1981 at the German Evangelical *Kirchentag* in Hamburg. On *Kirchentag*, see n. 6, p. 16.

1. Ita Ford and Maura Clark were Maryknoll sisters. Jean Donovan, a lay missioner, and Dorothy Kazel, an Ursuline sister, had been sent by the Diocese of Cleveland.

twenty-one, she joined the Maryknoll order. She went to Chile in 1973 just prior to the overthrow of Allende.[2] She was molded by the ensuing years of hardship and persecution; it was here that her commitment to the poor grew; it was here that she learned what it means to identify yourself as a Christian with the life of the poor, to live in a *barrio* with but few personal possessions, day and night available to intrusion by individuals in need of hiding places, food, clothing. In 1977 she reflected:

> Am I willing to suffer with the people here, the suffering of the powerless, the feeling impotent? Can I say to my neighbors—I have no solutions to this situation; I don't know the answers, but I will walk with you, search with you, be with you. Can I let myself be evangelized by this opportunity? Can I look at and accept my own poorness as I learn it from the other poor ones?

I want to make these thoughts of Ita Ford's my own. I would also like to "be evangelized by opportunity," as she puts it. I would like to regard the conditions of my life as opportunities to learn how one returns. I want to share feelings of impotence and powerlessness. I do not live in a slum among the poor but in one of the world's wealthiest countries which at the same time is one of the most highly armed. But we do share with others the experience of impotence to change anything, and our own poverty in terms of limitations and weakness is continuously brought home to us. Can I let this situation evangelize me, as Ita Ford asked herself? How can I, in our position, turn into a letter from Christ, an invitation to genuine living?

Perhaps the notes and letters of this nun and those of her fellow Maryknoller Maura Clark will one day be read in the Christian community in the same way we now read Dietrich

---

2. Salvador Allende Gossens (1908–73), the last elected (Marxist) president of Chile, assassinated during the 1973 military coup.

Bonhoeffer's letters and diaries.[3] Being a martyr means being a witness, a witness to truth, a witness to love, a witness to resistance and to voluntary surrender. Ita Ford could have led a rather different life, just like Bonhoeffer, who turned his back on security and a brilliant academic career in order to return to Nazi Germany. Ita Ford learned her lesson from the poor in Chile. When Archbishop Oscar Romero called for help in San Salvador, she felt challenged to go there.[4] Romero had just been assassinated when she arrived. The new beginning was not easy. She missed the other sisters and her friends. It was no simple matter to gain the trust of people who lived in constant fear, terrorized by the political situation. She worked for an emergency refugee project and wrote:

> I don't know if it is in spite of, or because of the horror, terror, evil, confusion, lawlessness—but I do know that it is right to be here . . . to believe that we are gifted in and for Salvador now, that the answers to the questions will come when they are needed, to walk in faith one day at a time with the Salvadoreans along a road filled with obstacles, detours, and sometimes washouts. . . .

Ita and her fellow sisters felt responsible to the needs of "the hurting, homeless, and hungry." They were quite aware of the political implications of feeding the hungry in a country caught up in a state of undeclared civil war. There were rumors that she had been put on the hit list of several rightist terror organizations. Toward the end of November, at Thanksgiving time, she attended the Maryknoll Regional Assembly in Nicaragua. The other sisters there reported that Ita seemed

3. Dietrich Bonhoeffer (1906–45)—German pastor, theologian, and teacher who was executed by the Nazis shortly before Allied forces reached the concentration camp where he had been held.

4. Oscar Arnulfo Romero y Galdames (1917–80), archbishop of San Salvador and public critic of human rights violations by a succession of governments in El Salvador, was assassinated while celebrating Mass.

to undergo a profound healing during those five days together. She had lost her closest friend and colleague in an accident early during her work in El Salvador. At the closing liturgy, Ita read from one of Oscar Romero's last sermons, a passage which foretold what would befall her less than twenty-four hours later:

fate of the poor

> Christ invites us not to fear persecution because, believe me, brothers and sisters, he who is committed to the poor must run the same fate as the poor, and in El Salvador we know what the fate of the poor signifies: to disappear, be tortured, to be captive—and to be found dead.

This death of four women has produced a glimmer of political hope in the mounting opposition of the Catholic church to the political and military intervention of the United States in El Salvador, an opposition found not only at the grass roots level but even in the bishops' conference.

In mid-January 1981, about fifteen hundred people participated in a liturgy at the White House, in Washington. It was a memorial service "for the four and the ten thousand" who were assassinated in El Salvador the previous year. Four white caskets were carried all the way to the Capitol, together with a huge symbolic coffin for the many other mostly defenseless victims, that is, for children, youth, *campesinos*, and women who were suspected as "subversive" or "terrorist," and executed.

Beyond the political hope there is a spiritual hope in which the life of people like Ita Ford is grounded. As Scripture enjoins: "It is by this that we know what love is: that Christ laid down his life for us. And we in turn are bound to lay down our lives for our brothers" (1 John 3:16). That is what Ita Ford did together with three others on 2 December 1980. If we wish to learn to live believably, we must listen to the voices of the poor and disenfranchised in the Third World.

In August 1980 Ita Ford wrote a birthday letter to her

sixteen-year-old niece Jennifer. A copy was given to me by one of the Maryknoll sisters and I want to quote from it in order to convey to you something of the spirit that bore up people such as Ita and Maura and Dorothy and Jean. Let us ask help from those who live and die believably:

Dear Jennifer,
    The odds that this note will arrive for your birthday are poor—but know I'm with you in April as you celebrate sixteen big ones. I hope it's a special day for you.
    I want to say something to you—and I wish I were there to talk to you—because sometimes, letters don't get across all the meaning and feeling. But I'll give it a try anyway.
    First of all, I love you and care about you and how you are. I'm sure you know that. And that holds if you're an angel or a goof-off, a genius or a jerk. A lot of that is up to you and what you decide to do with your life.
    What I want to say—some of it isn't too jolly birthday talk, but it's real. Yesterday I stood looking down at a 16 year old who had been killed a few hours earlier. I know of a lot of kids even younger who are dead. This is a terrible time in El Salvador for youth. A lot of idealism and commitment is getting snuffed out here now.
    The reasons why so many people are being killed are quite complicated—yet there are some clear, simple strands. One is that many people have found a meaning to live, to sacrifice, struggle and even die! And whether their life span is 16 years, 60 or 90, for them this life has had a purpose. In many ways they are fortunate people.
    Brooklyn is not passing through the drama of El Salvador, but some things hold true wherever one is—and at whatever age. What I'm saying is I hope you come to find that which gives life a deep meaning for you. Something worth living for—maybe even worth dying for—something that energizes you, enthuses you, enables you to keep moving ahead.
    I can't tell you what it might be—that's for you to find, to choose, to love. I can just encourage you to start looking and support you in the search.

This is how I understand this letter: no one can demonstrate your "believable life" or live it for you. Accommodation does not help. You yourself are responsible for the meaning you give your own life. You can give your life direction even if you are only sixteen. There is a Jewish saying that "the world has been created for the sake of choice by choosers." But many find themselves no longer in a position to choose between meaningless and meaningful work. They feel so trapped between the many pressures to consume that it hardly matters what they choose. Many feel that decisions about their life have long since been made elsewhere, that they function merely as programmed objects. In Ita Ford's letter to her sixteen-year-old niece I recognize a respect for life that will not permit anyone to have such low regard for him or herself. There is the pride of being a human being rather than a mere statistic. It is not true that our life is simply being lived for us. We can choose between a variety of options. It is possible to turn into a letter from Christ, written unto life, unto joy, and unto justice.

Some of you may well think, but we do not live in El Salvador. And we cannot all be missionaries or social workers. What use is this example of a Christian life? But I believe that this kind of thinking is subterfuge. It is thinking as though we did not wish to read the letter from Christ. Ita Ford does not tell her niece to leave Brooklyn, to become a nun, or to come to El Salvador. But she does challenge her to a different kind of life, different from what we would normally or fairly unconsciously submit to. And that is precisely the content of that letter from Christ that we could be. We could be an invitation to life, to be whole, to be authentic. Come, it says in that letter which we receive and which we are to be, it is a great good fortune to be alive, to be loved and to learn to love, to be treated justly and to stand for justice, to be appeased and to make peace. The kingdom of God is lived here and now—that is what it says in that letter from Christ which we are and shall more and more be.

If we are honest, we know that we can choose, that we have different options, that it does make a difference how we handle our time, our money, our energy. If we live credibly, we shall become ever more understandable to others. Then our hearts will radiate that bright glow, the reflection of God who brought forth light out of darkness. We are a letter from Christ. The message of the letter, its content, is inseparable from us. The medium is the message. We who may hope, who learn faith even while tempted to think too meanly of ourselves, we who are enabled to love even as we are afraid—we are the message, the letter from Christ, the invitation to life.

If you understand this in your heart, if you experience this unity with Christ in others and in yourself, then you will be sickened by the superficialities of Protestant politicians who argue that the church should confine itself to the nurture of souls and proclamation and leave politics to the politicians. They seem to be telling us: go ahead, be the letter from Christ as much and as long as you like, but no one may read it. You may carry the bright light in your heart, but no illumination, no discernment of God may be visible in public! The Sermon on the Mount is appropriate only to the private individual! We decide what peace means. I find such speeches offensive. They insult Amos and Jeremiah, they ridicule St. Francis and Martin Luther King, they know nothing of Dietrich Bonhoeffer or Ita Ford, and they perpetuate a notion of Christianity as banal as it is superficial.

Religion is not persecuted in our country. To believe in Father, Son, and Holy Spirit is permitted; it is permissible to attend church and to fulfill the so-called religious obligations. But as soon as faith impacts practical life—which includes politics, as Oscar Romero pointed out, meaning that faith must oppose the arms race as a crime against the poor—we are slandered as "naive" or "communist." Religious tolerance clearly is only skin deep; any living and genuine religiosity such as animated the women and men of the Confessing

Church[5] is undesired and suspect. In this society Christ does not, as conservative Christians would like, glorify and bless the culture. Christ stands opposed to this culture, to its barbarism and to its superficiality. He stands by the side of those who are victimized by this culture and who defy it. You cannot serve God and militarism. If you are not part of the solution, you are part of the problem.[6]

But what are we to do if we do not happen to live in a slum in El Salvador? To be blunt, I am growing ever more impatient with those who pose such a question. There is plenty to be done if you have opted for the poor, as Oscar Romero put it. You will find out. If your decision is serious, your priorities will change. Your life will have a purpose. Your needs will be different. You will no longer find it essential to throw out your furniture every three years. You will be involved in the struggle against hunger and injustice. You will find something worth living for, together with others, as a letter from Christ.

It is not a matter of politicizing and reorganizing an originally "purely religious" movement. Rather, here are people who are perplexed and scared in their total being, in everything that they think and feel. They fear this brutish prosperity in our land. They want to live differently. They want truth. They want to know why their country is being devastated, their trees cut down, their air poisoned, and who profits thereby. They seek justice, they want us to stop exploiting other peoples, once and for all. There is mounting resistance against the state that cannot cope with unemployment, the destruction of the environment, and a rising rate of suicides, and that at the same time embarks on the most extensive

5. Confessing Church—that part of the German Protestant churches that opposed the Nazi decrees and sought to remain faithful to Scripture and confessions, in contrast to the German Christian movement that adopted Nazi ideology.
6. The original text uses a rhymed German slogan—*Wer sich nicht wehrt, lebt verkehrt*—which means, "Who does not resist, lives all wrong."

military adventure in history. This resistance has profoundly religious roots. The yearning for a nonviolent life in justice simply cannot be eradicated.

Which Christ are the politicians willing to approve if they will not allow the one who preached the Sermon on the Mount? What religion will be deemed sensible if the one that wants to make peace without weaponry is ridiculed as naive? What relationship to truth can we imagine under the barrage of propaganda that camouflages the arms buildup as a "catching-up" and advertises annihilating holocaust as a "modernization of our arsenal"? How far can we carry love of neighbor under a government with a key interest in the ability to create a "credible threat" against each citizen of all our Eastern neighbors not nine, but eleven times over?

Is the letter from Christ which we are to remain illegible? Young people who seek something to which they can dedicate their lives, something more than career and affluence, are constantly discouraged, ridiculed, punished, and suppressed. "We have cause enough to weep even without your tear gas" was scrawled on the walls of their city by young people in Zürich.[7] They feel a deep need to live authentically, and they have every right to demand more than the tired old script of the so-called do-able.[8] They stand in the best of Judaic and Christian tradition with their criticism and their desire to rethink everything. For this tradition has ever spoken of returning, of transformation, of conversion. It never asked: What is do-able? but: What is just? What is the will of God in any given situation? The tradition has always insisted that we are able to know what is just, that we have been told what God

7. Not only Switzerland, but all of Europe was shaken when young people rampaged in Zürich and other Swiss cities. Switzerland had always been regarded as the most stable of countries, with its high level of participatory electoral democracy (at least for males).

8. *Das Machbare*, the do-able (the expedient), was a phrase popularized by Helmut Schmidt when he was chancellor of Germany.

wants of us, that we are capable of truth. If we were to give up that quest and only want to find out what is expedient, then we would betray the biblical tradition.

If I listen carefully to the protesting young people, what they seem to be telling me is: The do-able is death. If you are content with the expedient, you destroy your own capacity for renewal and thinking new thoughts. You will be caught up in routine functioning, with life merely running down the program reel. I know this condition all too well from periods of stress and overextension. I shall try to describe it so that you will recognize it and will understand why I say that the do-able means death. I am then withdrawn even from myself to the extent that my skin is no longer sensitive to touch. I no longer feel anything. I am no longer my body, just physical mass. . . . I carry on whatever is essential quite mechanically. My movements are dead. Nothing brings joy, nothing brings sorrow. Nothing really reaches me. I eat without being hungry. I gorge information that I do not need. I am not alive; some machine has taken me over. I am dead, not as a human being who has died but as a computer that never lived. Mystics have called this condition a "drought of the soul." It is existing without water, without greenery, without shade, without reference, without prospect. It is an existence oriented to doing and the do-able, where nothing thrives or flourishes. I think most people know this sense of isolation and being-turned-into-a-machine quite well. We are a machine for work, an eating machine, a sex machine, a reading machine, a purchasing machine. In Christian tradition such devastated existence is known as "living without God." Many make themselves comfortable that way and no longer even notice that the do-able is death. Others, such as those young people in Zürich, "have plenty of reason to cry, even without your tear gas." There are solid reasons to weep over unemployed, uneducated youth without a future. But I hear something more in this cry: A longing that arises out of despair over the so-called do-able for a return to a genuine life. Yes, we do have much reason to weep. Such are the tears that Christ wept over Jerusalem.

In order to make progress, we must change direction and return. In order to learn, we must first of all unlearn. In order to remain alive, we must be born again. In order to find meaning, we must change our mind. Turn about! Choose a different road! Challenge the goals that have become so accepted that they are never questioned anymore. Review your life style, which is so deeply embedded that we no longer even notice its routine. Life is a returning, is conversion. Living means turning about; dully to stay the course just because we once embarked on it, means to die. The scale of values in our society is based on the model of continuous progress. A car is better if it can reach higher speeds, the grape harvest is superior if there are more grapes, an atomic missile is better if it can destroy more accurately. This scale glorifies technological progress.

Christianity proclaims not progress but a returning. The most direct route does not continue in the familiar direction, but calls for turning-about-on-your-heel and repudiating phony goals and life-destroying expectations. Turning and conversion is not a once-and-for-all act in a person's life, but a daily exercise to extricate ourselves from the heavy armor which we ourselves put on.

Without a change in the direction of our lives, everything will continue as before. We shall continue to pursue the aims to which we have become accustomed, we shall cling to what we have, we shall run in the same direction blind to everything that is happening about us and deaf to the voices of those whose life we destroy. I mean the poor, as threatened by starvation as ever, and I mean the next generation whom we expect to live with our atomic garbage and a biosphere we shall have destroyed.

I read about returning in the prophet Jeremiah:

> "If you return, O Israel, says the Lord,
>   to me you should return.
> If you remove your abominations from my presence,
>   and do not waver,
> and if you swear, 'As the Lord lives,'
>   in truth, in justice, and in uprightness,
> then nations shall bless themselves in him,
>   and in him shall they glory."
> For thus says the Lord to the men of Judah and to the
> inhabitants of Jerusalem:
> "Break up your fallow ground,
>   and sow not among thorns." (Jer. 4:1–3)

Whoever sows under hedges and among thorns will stifle life. It cannot grow. Many try to avoid a returning and to muddle along as usual. It is an attempt not to change the abominations, the misdeeds of which the prophet speaks, not to abandon them, but to carry on, perhaps a trifle more moderately. In our situation that would mean to insist on further industrial growth, to plan for higher consumption of energy, and above all to lust after more military security.

Around the turn of the century a single injustice committed against a Jewish officer provoked an immense wave of sympathy, revulsion, and protest in France. I am referring to the Dreyfus affair which provided one impetus for the founding of the League for Human Rights.[9] Toward the end of our century, injustice that cries unto heaven is perpetrated daily and hourly against millions of people whose only fault is to have been born with the wrong skin color or on the wrong continent. Most of us in the Western world have become used to that. We have become machines to such a degree that it no longer bothers us.

We still call this condition under which we live peace, just

9. Alfred Dreyfus (1859–1935), accused falsely of treason and convicted in 1893, retried and convicted but pardoned in 1899. The verdict was reversed in 1906 after a huge public outcry, including Emile Zola's famous 1901 *j'accuse* pamphlet.

as we refer to the arms race as preparation, just in case. But in
reality we live already in the midst of a ghastly war, the war of
the rich against the poor, a war carried on by economic means
under military protection. Every day there are thousands of
casualties in this war; they die of hunger and other entirely
curable diseases. The American peace movement characterizes this fact with a simple slogan: The bombs are falling now.
The arms race is not just preparation for a military conflict of
the future, but it is the war in which we are already engaged
and in which fifteen thousand people die each day because
there is no food for them. The condition of absolute poverty is
not caused by lack of natural resources or by a factor such as
overpopulation, but by the economic warfare carried on by
the North against the South. The bombs we produce are
falling now—on the poor.

Turn about! Break up your fallow ground! From what must
we convert, and to what? I think that can be said in simple
words: The system under which we live is based on money
and power. Money and power are the highest goals. I remember a minor incident in an elite German high school where a
boy was asked about his career plans half a year before gradua-
tion. He was not really quite sure yet, he said, the main thing
was to earn plenty. This was a notably honest remark. Just
about that time, the *Frankfurter Allgemeine Zeitung* published an advertisement entitled: "Put a quarter of what you
made in gold into arms production!"[10] To support this, the ad
continued: "America is increasing military procurement by
fifteen billion dollars! That is the kickoff. Sooner or later
orders will be placed to match this, that is, there will be a
matching arms buildup in NATO countries and in other countries. Fifty billion dollars . . . that is the current estimate for
the total increase in Western military budgets." Since this will

10. FAZ (*Frankfurter Allgemeine Zeitung*), one of Germany's most re-
spected and quoted daily newspapers.

place the armaments industry "on a wholly new basis of earning power," the advertisement recommended the purchase of stock in first-class corporations active in the arms trade.

I report these two stories of the graduate who wants to earn money above all and of the advertisement that urges financial speculation in arms production in order to throw light on what the well-to-do in our society plan and desire. Obviously, there is a connection between money and power. Objectively, it hardly matters to that young man whether he makes his money in business or by speculating in real estate. And objectively speaking, the advertisement that points out the current best investment opportunity is quite accurate. The do-able is death. Money and power are inseparable. Our affluence is a brutal thing and therefore has to be protected by ever greater force and terror. We are all caught up in this dominance of money and violence, even if it is only by not even fully admitted desires to share a little of the money and the power. How can we liberate ourselves from this domination? How can we become a letter from Christ in which the poor can find hope and not a new threat? How can we return and cease to honor the idols of money and power? We do not live in El Salvador, and yet we can hear the voices of the poor. The most important message which we as Christians in the Federal Republic of Germany (West Germany) must hear is the message of the poor, their accusations and their proposals for more just distribution. The antiracism program of the World Council of Churches, which supports liberation movements, provides one example of how we as congregations can listen to the poor. Those who have attempted this in recent years have been drawn more and more into the concerns and hopes of the poor. In this way we allow ourselves to be evangelized by the poor and shall be turning away from the idols of our own society. When the poor turn into the letter from Christ to us, then we shall return and seek authentic life. Then we shall begin to love God rather than money and power.

When I talk about loving God I mean something entirely concrete which you can all see and experience here at the *Kirchentag.* That is the peace movement, this great hope for a returning of our people, this clear revival in our nation, a turning away from money and the violence which is supposed to safeguard our affluence, and a turning to God who gives life. Conversion is not something to which churches call other people by preaching to them. It is something happening right here, before our eyes. People who have been asleep and kept silent long enough, who allowed themselves to be manipulated and were as the dead under the coercive rule of money and power, are rising up for peace and against that most brutal form of power which rules over us, the nuclear arms race.

I must tell you honestly that I would not have thought that such liberation and life could spring from the church, this evangelical church in West Germany which I have experienced so often as a tomb of Christ.[11] But if God can create out of stones sons and daughters who agitate for peace, why not out of the congregations?

A few years ago many of the most thoughtful people I know longed to be in the Third World because there the struggles were straightforward, the lines more clearly drawn, the hopes more immediate. "I wish I were in Nicaragua," a student wrote to me, "There it would be possible to live as a Christian." To many of us it seemed as if one could find Christ only at the side of the poor and not in a "first world" context. I suspect that that has rather changed now. We do not live in El Salvador, but under the rule of NATO. In their planning offices they make decisions about our lives and those of other nations. That is where false idols are raised and that is where

11. "Evangelical church" normally simply means Protestant in German usage. Collectively it means primarily the various Lutheran, Reformed, and United regional churches, as well as so-called "free churches."

our battle lies. Our historical task is the fight for peace and against militarism. That is how we may participate in the liberation struggles of the Third World.

Nowadays, no one who feels solidarity with the poor still has cause to despair or to engage in senseless acts of destruction or self-destruction. Since the December 1979 NATO decision which is intended to establish the permanent rule of terror, we have known where to find our El Salvador, our Vietnam, our Soweto, our liberation struggle, and our conversion from money and violence to justice and peace.

When I first heard the watchword of this *Kirchentag* I was a bit confused. I had always been taught that in using the Bible you have to be alert to who is being addressed. Who then is being addressed in the Bible with this "Be not afraid"? Above all, surely, those who are treated unjustly, who have been driven from their homes, who are poor and in danger, deserted or scared are addressed. Those who suffer injustice are addressed, not those who profit from it, and those who are under threat from any enemy, not those eager to create "a credible threat," as our security experts put it, against other peoples. When I looked up the passages where the comforting "Fear not" appears, I almost always found it in conjunction with words that emphasized the reestablishment of right and justice. If our *Kirchentag* were being held in Northern Brazil, for instance, or in Taiwan, or in the black ghetto of South Africa, if would make good sense. Then the people there could hear what the prophet Isaiah has to say to them:

> Strengthen the weak hands,
>   and make firm the feeble knees.
> Say to those who are of a fearful heart,
>   "Be strong, fear not!
> Behold, your God will come with vengeance, with the
> recompense of God.
>   He will come and save you."
> Then the eyes of the blind shall be opened,

and the ears of the deaf unstopped;
then shall the lame man leap like a hart,
    and the tongue of the dumb sing for joy.
For waters shall break forth in the wilderness,
    and streams in the desert;
the burning sand shall become a pool,
    and the thirsty ground springs of waters.

(Isa. 35:3–7)

That is a text for a people in exile. A text for the poor, not for the rich. Is it a text for us as well? Is it a consolation also for us? The answer to this question is straightforward: yes, provided we stand on the side of the poor; yes, if we hear their cry and take up their demand, until the last medium-range missile has been turned into plowshares or tractors, into rural health clinics and irrigation projects. On the side of the poor in the war that our own class carries out against them, God speaks to us: Fear not! They will come with clubs, and gas, and dogs—but be not afraid. Behold your God. Water shall break forth in the wilderness.

Fear not!
The rulers can no longer avoid the writing on the wall
their subjects have ceased nodding their heads
the arms merchants no longer dare climb over those prostrate
    on the ground
bishops give up on slippery words and say no
the friends of Jesus are blocking the streets of overkill
school children are learning the truth
how shall we recognize an angel
but that he gives courage
where there was fear
joy where even grief no longer thrived
intervention where coercion ruled
disarmament where terror menaced credibly
fear not, resistance rises.

6

TEN YEARS OF PRISON FOR DANIEL BERRIGAN*

America is not only the land of Ronald Reagan and his neutron bomb. There is another America. There, too, you will find a movement for peace and against militarism. There is resistance, and we could learn from it here.

Recently, the well-known Jesuit Father Daniel Berrigan was sentenced to ten years in prison, his brother Philip to three years. In September 1980, a group of eight nonviolent resistance fighters entered a General Electric plant that produces nuclear missile parts. Among those entering were a Catholic nun and a mother of six children. They damaged two missile nose cones with hammers and poured human blood, their own, according to the report, over drawings, plans, and equipment. Overpowered by military police, they were handed over to the local police force and arrested. The charges were burglary, criminal conspiracy, criminal trespass, incitement to riot, disturbing the peace (the prosecutors probably were referring to the singing of religious peace hymns), larceny, and coercion. The damage they had done was estimated at between ten and thirty thousand dollars.

The accused declared:

We commit civil disobedience at General Electric because this genocidal entity is the fifth leading producer of weaponry in the U.S.A. To maintain this position, General Electric drains three million dollars a day from the public treasury, an enormous larceny against the poor. . . . Through the Mark 12A reentry

*Broadcast of Germany's Southwest Radio in Baden-Baden, 13 October 1981, in the series *Blick in die Zeit* ("Looking at Our Age").

vehicle, the threat of first-strike nuclear war grows more immi-
nent. Thus, General Electric advances the possible destruction
of millions of innocent lives. . . . we choose to obey God's law of
life, rather than a corporate summons to death. Our beating of
swords into plowshares today is a way to enflesh this biblical
call.

Well, for this faithfulness to the prophet Isaiah and to the
Sermon on the Mount, which calls the peacemakers blessed,
the Plowshares Eight, as the group has biblically named itself,
have been given prison sentences reminiscent of military dic-
tatorships such as that in Korea. During the Vietnam War the
Berrigan brothers were repeatedly in jail because they pub-
licly napalmed draft records, burning them under the motto
"burn files, not children." In 1970 Daniel Berrigan had noted
that Americans who can bear the sight of burning children
with equanimity are infuriated out of their minds at the sight
of burning files. In a way, radical Catholic pacifists regard
prison as the appropriate place for Christians to find themselves in this period of preparation of nuclear holocaust. Their
notions of resistance were drawn from the Bible, from
Gandhi, from European and German resistance to Hitler.
Dietrich Bonhoeffer, theologian of the resistance against
Hitler and who was hanged by the Nazis, is one model for
them. They formulate their political convictions this way: Our
enemy is not the Soviets, but the bomb. In the face of the
renewed American arms buildup, Philip Berrigan has suggested that we must take greater risks than ever before.

Daniel Berrigan is a friend of mine. Most recently he
worked in a hospice for cancer patients. He visits them,
consoles them, prays with them, celebrates mass with them.
To the question: "Why do you work in a hospice for terminally
ill cancer patients? Is that not a distraction from your actions
against the arms race?" he responds:

Let me say first that I need to do some kind of physical work
with people who suffer. In that way you can find out the

meaning of death by cancer. Nowadays, in the world of the bomb, that seems to me to be an appeal to human beings. It is a calling for humanity. It is the burning image of human life itself: to experience those cancer victims is a test for the future as that is being planned now. To be with individuals who are dying of cancer is to be among those on whom the bomb has already fallen. And that is a great privilege. The people in our care, the experience of that suffering, help me to find my path to the Pentagon and to the White House and to those places where our communities meet to resist a future of death and cancer.[1]

Besides, Daniel Berrigan the poet goes to prison where there are mostly young black inmates, and he teaches them to write poetry and prose. His health is not exactly robust; I can hardly imagine that he would survive ten years of imprisonment. Why such a severe sentence for an internationally known nonviolent pacifist? What are the United States and its judicial organs afraid of? Is this a preemptive attempt to neutralize the leadership of a peace movement that is regaining its strength? Benjamin Spock, the well-known pediatrician, commited a similar outrage of civil disobedience in the White House in May 1981 and was briefly under arrest. Is that other America still alive, that America which did, after all, contribute significantly to bringing genocide in Vietnam to an end? More importantly, is there a younger generation in the United States with something in their heads other than money and business and a military establishment to protect this affluence? Resistance and resistors are ever more important words there. They signify that an increasing number of people are standing up and acting fearlessly, nonviolently, and militantly against the madness that has befallen those who rule over us. The tradition of civil disobedience is relatively unknown in

1. This response by Daniel Berrigan and the one that follows shortly are translations from interviews published in German. Father Berrigan's discussions of these points in English are widely available, some of them in reports of the trial testimony.

Germany, as is that of symbolic action. During one such action in Washington, D.C., blood was splashed against the columns, the entrances, and walls of the Pentagon.

I quote from an interview. To the question, "Why do you employ such symbols?" Berrigan responded:

> We are dealing with the handicapped, in the case of the Pentagon, with the mentally handicapped. We are not negotiating with a rational power. That is why we cannot use rational means of communication alone—leaflets, discussion, but also a-rational ones, that is, symbols. Symbols to make death real. Generals never see the other side of their decisions. There is a deep chasm between the decision and its consequence. It is dreadful to see human blood in the corridors of the Pentagon. Nothing is more dreadful for the people who have been called into this giant Greek temple. Suddenly the truth of our situation is in the air and under our feet, and that is awful. For us— for most of us are Christians—this simply means a broadening of our regular worship service. Our tradition is sacred to us. It is full of symbols: human blood, ashes, water, oil. We see it this way: we are taking the body and the blood from the altar and carrying them to the Pentagon. In the same way Christ was brought from the Last Supper to Golgotha, in a single day.

These Catholic pacifists commit civil disobedience to be obedient to God. They destroy furnishings and equipment that serve to prepare murder, in order to protect life. And while Reagan approves for mass production that new bomb that merely kills people and leaves things and structures intact, to be used by the victor, Daniel Berrigan and his friends go to prison for the sake of human dignity, "Made in U.S.A."

Perhaps we shall see the day when prisons will be overcrowded with peace marchers to the point where judges can no longer criminalize the love of peace, where generals regain the capacity to learn, and where bankers will no longer advocate speculation in arms production as the best available investment. In that sense, Daniel Berrigan, every day that you spend in jail of those up to ten years is a gift to each one of us, a bit of truth and a consolation. Peace can be isolated by deadly silence—that is what the American media are attempting to do, followed most obediently here by the German media. But you cannot beat peace to death: peace is with you in prison, with you, within you. The peace of Christ even in a prison in Norristown, Pennsylvania, U.S.A.

7

THERE IS
ANOTHER AMERICA*

Dear friends of peace, there is another America! The United States is not simply the land of Ronald Reagan and Alexander Haig; for the resistance which grows daily here among us also grows on the other side of the Atlantic. No one should imagine that a crime such as nuclear arms development, a preparation of aggressive war, or the planning of limited atomic war could be carried out entirely behind the backs of all the nations involved as if they were completely powerless and disenfranchised! Just remember the resistance of the American people against the Vietnam War. That was the time when I learned to love the American people: these hundreds of thousands of young and older folk, of women and men, of diverse races, who spoke a clear "no" to the genocide in southeast Asia with courage and shrewdness, with imagination and "civil valor,"[1] with resistance and civil disobedience. Because of them the United States could not carry out the war with the even greater military brutality required by a politics of total annihilation. In this way the opposition within America contributed to the victory of the Vietnamese people! "Suppose they gave a war and no one came!" Something like that actually occurred: fewer and fewer wanted to come. This other America has not died! As we stand here protesting against the man who gathered the most important experiences of his life

*Speech given 19 September 1981 at a rally protesting then U.S. Secretary of State Alexander Haig's visit to Berlin.
1. A much-quoted phrase taken from Chancellor Bismarck's assertion that Germans lacked "civil courage" or "civil valor."

as an official of United Technologies, one of the world's largest arms producers, there is a concurrent demonstration by an antiwar mobilization in Detroit, where one hundred thousand are expected to represent the true interests of the American people. There is an America of the poor, of blacks, of Puerto Ricans, of women. There is the interest of the poor, of 27 million people who live below the poverty level in the richest country of the world, the interest of the more than fifty percent of black youth in the ghettos who cannot find work, of the old, of welfare recipients.

Robert F. Drinan,[2] a Jesuit on the faculty of Georgetown University in Washington, D.C., commenting on the Reagan budget, concluded: all the poor will be poorer. That is precisely what U.S. Secretary of Defense Caspar Weinberger suggests the German government also do: make all the poor poorer. The economic interests of the poorest, of the poor, and of the lower middle class are crushed underfoot. As the well-to-do have their taxes reduced, 32 billion dollars are cut from earlier food stamp programs, school lunches, rent subsidies, and job training.

Politically, too, there is another America besides the one represented by Mr. Haig. It is not sufficiently known in Germany that Reagan's election victory was based on the vote of only twenty-eight percent of Americans registered to vote. And one-half of eligible Americans do not even register to vote. People have lost hope that anything can be changed by voting, and they do not recognize that by not voting matters are made worse. But it is precisely among those who no longer expect to be able to alter their condition through the parliamentary electoral process that political resistance is mounting against militarism, an economic crime in the first degree against the poor within the country as well as worldwide.

2. Former dean of the law school at Boston College and later congressman from Massachusetts.

I want to say something about the new shape of resistance against the arms race. It is a little easier for Americans than for us, inasmuch as their government propaganda is more open and cynical than ours in Europe. In American public life no one hears of the so-called "double-track decision." There is no question of negotiations; there is a commitment to the arms race without ifs and buts. The word *Nachrüstung* is an untranslatable German linguistic casuistry. In the United States it is clear that America must once again be number one, the leading world power, and this new slogan is understood in primarily military terms. Superiority is the new goal, no longer are the goals parity and the balance of terror.

I want to mention a few examples of resistance. There are native Americans in the southwest who are fighting yet once again against being driven from their land, against the rape of their mineral rights, and the theft of their water. There are Mormons in Utah opposing the basing of the MX missiles in their state. There is every indication that this opposition will be successful: the environmental costs would be excessive.

There is, secondly, the anti-imperialist resistance to U.S. intervention in El Salvador. We can thank the peace and civil rights movement that El Salvador has not yet been entirely Vietnamized. Latin America is closer to the heart of most North Americans than is Europe. Therefore, much of the kind of organizing that has occurred in Europe against the proposed arms buildup by NATO and the militarization of our society has occurred in the United States against the suppression of liberation movements in Central and South America. For it has been the dedication of various U.S. administrations to maintain an economic system that is based on the exploitation and continued pauperization of peoples in the Third World. The mounting military aid for the junta in El Salvador has met with fierce resistance, especially among American Christians. The fact that it was American bullets that were used in the murder of the four American religious women in December 1980 has not yet been forgotten.

Thirdly, there is the resistance of the churches against nuclear arms development. This, in fact, goes far beyond what we could expect here in our wildest dreams from our bishops and church leaders. The Conference of Superiors of Catholic Orders, the United States Catholic Bishops Conference, and the Protestant National Council of Churches have spoken out clearly against the neutron bomb. We may no longer refer to that weapon as "controversial" on the North German Radio Network (NDR)! The Roman Catholic archbishop of Seattle, Raymond G. Hunthausen, has spoken out for unilateral steps toward disarmament and for nonviolent resistance to the nuclear arms race.

One of the measures suggested by Archbishop Hunthausen is to refuse to pay fifty percent of one's federal income tax. In addressing the six hundred delegates to the 1981 convention in Tacoma, Washington, of the Lutheran Church in America Pacific Northwest Synod, he said: "I am told by some that unilateral disarmament in the face of atheistic communism is insane." Then he added: "I find myself observing that nuclear armament by anyone is itself atheistic, and anything but sane."

Leroy Matthiesen, the archbishop of Amarillo, Texas, in addressing employees of the Pentax Corporation who are working on the neutron bomb, suggested that they should refuse that work, even if it meant being fired; the church would help them find peaceful work. Bishop George Ivens of Denver, Colorado led a march of five thousand demonstrators to the plutonium enrichment facility at Rocky Flats.

There is another America! The resistance of women: within the women's movement there is a growing realization that the very same system that cheats women out of a fully human life also produces neutron bombs. Thousands of women have encircled the Pentagon. They noted that every day, while they

work, study, and love, these colonels and generals who plan
our destruction calmly walk through the doors of the five sides
of the Pentagon. Eighty of these women were arrested in
1980.

These forms of protest, including the one hundred thousand Mobilization Members that stood at the north side of the
Pentagon on 3 May 1981, are totally blacked out by our
media, as is almost all of the internal resistance movement in
America. We do not hear about this protest, and nothing of
the suffering, the incarceration, and the persecution of those
women who resist. But more and more women understand
that the world we want to build, the new sharing of life
together we seek, is threatened by nothing as much as by the
militarism of the men who rule. Once you have understood
what it means to be a woman, you belong on the side of peace
and not among those who want to secure it unto death! This
realization is surging ahead within the American women's
movement.

The Catholic Workers' movement has constantly produced
new nonviolent actions. Daniel Berrigan and others damaged
two nuclear missile nose cones; they poured blood over the
blueprints of mass murder. Father Berrigan has been sentenced to prison for up to ten years. The sentence for this
internationally renowned Christian pacifist is so severe that it
reminds you of Korea. I believe that we can learn more about
the intellectual, human, and political significance of the
United States in the current world from Daniel Berrigan, who
protests the system which he simply calls "the bomb," than
we can from the official civil servant of death who is a guest in
this city today. Years ago Daniel Berrigan said that through his
experiences he hoped to inspire others to devise alternatives
to the killing, to the socializing of killing, to the technologiz-
ing of killing. As we stand here today as a living alternative to
killing, to the learning to kill, and to obedience unto death,
we are close to that other, the true America.

We are not the ones who are anti-American; it is Mr. Haig and his friends who contradict all the great democratic traditions of the United States. Let me quote an earlier president of the United States, Abraham Lincoln, who in 1858 posed this question in an election debate: "What constitutes the bulwark of our own liberty and independence? It is not our frowning battlements, . . . the guns of our war steamers, or the strength of our . . . army. These are not our reliance against a resumption of tyranny in our fair land. All of them may be turned against our liberties. . . ."3 What Jefferson and Lincoln meant by democracy had nothing to do with the urge to be number one and the ability to subjugate others, or with the alleged rights of the economically superior.

Perhaps this is a good moment to remember one of the greatest historical challenges of the American people, the institution of slavery. Slavery and nuclear arms are comparable phenomena. The advocates of slavery thought it an economic necessity, just as certain military strategists today regard war for economic reasons, for instance, to safeguard oil supplies, as defensible, possibly even as necessary. The advocates of slavery did intend to reform the conditions of slavery and humanize them just as the advocates of nuclear arms today plead for limited nuclear war, small neutron bombs, and so on. The advocates of slavery thought it quite natural that there had always been slaves. They could not imagine life without slavery, just as the arms racers nowadays regard life without weapons as impossible.

History tells us that slavery was abolished, at least as a legal institution, through long struggles. We have come here because we believe that that other slavery, the arms race under which we live, will someday be abolished if it does not kill us first. The slave traders who still rule over us now will then no

3. From a speech given at Edwardsville, Illinois, 11 September 1858, during Lincoln's campaign for the U.S. Senate against Judge and Senator Stephen Arnold Douglas (1813–61)

longer be received with high honors and greeted as the representatives of another people. Atomic arsenals will then be regarded by the majority just as slavery is, as irrational and contrary to our own interests! It runs just as much against the best interests of the majority of the American people. The arms race is morally as unacceptable as the slavery of another people. It is not natural unless we regard it as natural to give in to the darkest instincts of subjugation, of menace and of killing. One of these days, slave traders will be treated as they deserve.

It is not us, the peace movement, who are anti-American. What is anti-American, if that phrase still has any meaning, is atomic slavery which turns our country into a launching pad and a prime target and condemns our citizens to be atomic hostages or victims. There is another America besides that of United Technologies, of General Electric, of the Nixons and Reagans. There is another America besides the one that produced the catastrophes of Nagasaki and My Lai and the consequent tradition in which Alexander Haig thinks and acts. The slave system was overcome historically thanks to that other America, and atomic slavery can be overcome. Thus far our century has failed in its task to outlaw war just as slavery was outlawed. In this task we stand squarely in and for the best American traditions, we find ourselves in solidarity with people in resistance in the United States; as they do, we seek a government of the people and not one of the wealthy minority, a government by the people and not by businessmen and specialists in atomic weapons, and a government for the people. A government of the people, by the people, and for the people. It is part of the best American tradition to recognize that slavery is equally intolerable for the slave and for the master. Abraham Lincoln said: "As I would not be a *slave*, so I would not be a *master*. This expresses my idea of democracy."[4]

4. From a fragment, 1 August 1858.

Today we do not wish to be slaves of the atomic lobby, of atomic research, of atomic technology. We do not wish to live as if everything do-able also needs to be done. We do not want to be masters in the system of atomic slavery, or victors in a limited atomic war, or blackmailers in total arms development.

How can we move from the condition of slavery in which we currently find ourselves into that of freedom from atomic weapons? The road cannot be that of negotiation and bilateral agreement; the last thirty years have proved that. We must begin to disarm, here and now, unilaterally. We do not wish to be either slaves or masters, but to abolish slavery. The specific demands for this are:

> No medium-range missiles in Europe.
> No neutron weapons.
> A nuclear-weapons-free zone in Europe.

Who can enforce this if not those who enjoy a little more freedom, that is, the inhabitants of the Western democracies? The difference between the West and East is not in the number of tanks, medium-range missiles, or in mutual assurances of overkill. The difference is in the live movement for peace which can speak out loudly here even though harrassed. Who then could initiate the attempt to achieve more peace if not those who have a little more peace? In this, too, we are in agreement with that other America—that more democracy means more capacity for peace, that more participation in what determines our lives gives us a capacity for peace. How did Lincoln put it? Our strength is not in "frowning battlements, . . . war steamers, or the strength of our army," not in "Corpus Christi," "Trident," and neutron weapons; our strength has been in the measure of democracy we have attained. When it is no longer NATO that decides how a meadow is to be used by the local residents, when it is no longer the minister of defense who determines what is to be taught in schools but the community of teachers and students, then we shall be neither masters nor slaves. Our idea of democracy aims to create more liberty and more peace, a pacifist democracy that creates peace—in solidarity with that other America.

8

WHEN A RIVER
TIPS OVER*

Atomic death does not threaten only those who are afraid, but also those who feel more secure with atomic death at hand. The arms race kills even without war. When a river tips over, what happens is this: the amount of pollution passes the critical point below which the life chain is sustainable. Fish die, plants follow them, the water stinks. When a river tips over, it is no longer really a river but a sewage drain. And what if a country tips over? What if the pernicious and poisonous substance becomes so omnipresent that life is choked off, that people despair of the possibility of living here, when they seek to emigrate or go to pieces, when they float about like fish in the stinking broth? When a river is ecologically polluted it tips over. When a country is militaristically polluted and arms itself to death, that country will tip over.

Just imagine peace were to break out. Not the peace of the brutes who calculate the megadead in advance, not the peace of rising dividends and stock values of corporations with weapons contracts, not the peace of the blacklisting of professional persons who are supposed to be a defense risk (and aren't we all?), not peace at the expense of the poor and at the cost of torture in Turkey. I do not mean that peacelessness that governs our land.

Suppose the people were to explain peace to the government: what it really means, peace. Suppose the government were finally to understand and explain it to the Americans.

*Speech given at the Bonn peace rally of 10 October 1981.

We forgo your protection. We shall leave the alliance. We do not want to let ourselves be armed to death by you. Half the money earmarked for holocaust preparation we shall need for problems in our country, for housing, for health and schools, and for all the foreigners who are not allowed schooling here. The other half we shall put into peaceful Third World projects, to fight the root causes of hunger. The arms trade will be banned immediately and companies that deal in it will be treated as the criminals they are.

Just imagine peace were to break out. We in the heart of Europe would be defenseless. We would no longer practice war, learn war, play war, or pay for war with our taxes. We would in no way be a threat to our neighbors. No one—not even the *Neues Deutschland*[1]—could accuse us of aggression, peacelessness, preparation of aggressive war, or first strike dreams. For the first time in our country's history we would be free: free from the desire to kill, to take revenge, or to kill as a precaution. We would have abolished the slavery under which humanity has labored to this day—the slavery of war and atomic slavery. And just imagine this true liberty: not to threaten or to cheat anyone, not to lie or blackmail. It means freedom from the necessity of preparing for a crime the like of which has never yet occurred in human history, the atomic destruction of all life. It means to be free from the preparation for murder and suicide.

Just imagine we were disarmed. We would be living in a peaceful country. Would we be invaded? Would we be the vacuum that would pull in an aggressive enemy like a magnet? No one can answer this question with certainty. I do not regard it as likely that the Soviet Union would attack such a Germany, but there is a risk and a residue of fear which we cannot talk people out of. But the question is whether this risk

1. "New Germany"—the major national newspaper of the German Democratic Republic (East Germany).

and this fear are not considerably less than what we currently undergo. Does not the preparation of a first strike by which we could turn the European part of the Soviet Union into a field of rubble and corpses in four minutes—does not such preparation constitute a greater risk and a greater danger for us than the peaceful third path that we seek?

Just imagine peace were to break out. Not an armed, enforced peace, but the peace free of violence which we have advocated and for the sake of which we will not use violent means, because the means of the struggle would cripple the aim of the struggle. We may only use nonviolent means to prepare the peace we seek. We mistrust the government precisely because it intends to safeguard peace by the most violent method in history—mass annihilation. Their method, an arms buildup, contradicts their goal, disarmament. Their method, violence, atomic violence, contradicts their wish, security. We want to hold together the ends and the means of our life.

Just imagine we could make it fully clear to the government why we have come here. We could share our vision, our dream, with them. We could remind the desperate arms racers of what they really intend and we could unmask the cynical arms racers so that anyone could see what their real interests are. What, after all, is the difference between East and West? It is not the difference between SS–20s and Pershing IIs; don't let them pull the wool over your eyes! The real difference between East and West is us, the peace movement, the fact that they are arming in the East without the people being able to raise their voices.

Just imagine the spirit of disarmament, of vulnerability, becoming clearly manifest so that our dream would become real: liberation from slavery, a banning of the slave traders, the greatest historical task of human beings on this planet toward the end of the twentieth century. Perhaps we would end up a little poorer. I think most of us would be glad to pay the price.

Perhaps we shall have to do a little more for this peace of which we dream than travel to Bonn. Perhaps we need to practice how to say no, the major and the many minor refusals in the hospital, in the barracks, at work, and school. We have a totally one-sided viewpoint, one-sidedly for life and against death, one-sided against the tools of mass destruction, which cannot be called weapons any more than the gas in Auschwitz deserved to be called a "weapon." We are not partly for death and partly for life, not for the death of others and for our own survival: we stand here because we love life whole, undivided, and as vulnerable as it happens to be.

Ronald Reagan has recently spoken of a window of vulnerability that he wants to close. The window in our country is still open. We can still have some light enter our reason and breathe some air into our lungs. Reagan and the weapons builders who claim to be his friends want to brick up that window. But without light and without air we should wither, we should suffocate. God created us vulnerable—that means capable of peace.

9

UNILATERALLY FOR PEACE*

December 12, 1979 was a black day in the history of Europe and of the world. The decision by leaders of NATO to participate obediently in American arms deployment policy constitutes a significant change for all our lives. In the future, perhaps, the era prior to December 1979 will be referred to as "the post-World War II period" and the time after December 1979 as "pre-World War III," in case anybody will be referring to anything after that. What happened? The decision in favor of a new nuclear arms race through medium-range missiles involves the *preparation of an aggressive war.* The unthinkable becomes thinkable. The "balance of terror," which was frightening enough, has run its course. The world power that wants to become number one once again is seeking nuclear superiority through which a limited nuclear war appears possible, conductable, and winnable.

The mendacity of militaristic language has often been noted. "Counterattack" refers to the preemptive destruction of hostile nuclear weapons before a war has actually begun. If the population has to be atomically destroyed, it is called "countervalue"; if nonmilitary targets are threatened, they speak of "counterforce." Using the "counter" terminology is supposed to emphasize one's defensive and veil one's aggressive character—that is the most critical linguistic game of arms race propaganda. Counterforce is a strategy that is about as much a matter of "defense" as was Hitler's attack on Poland

*Reprinted from *Mut zur Angst. Schriftsteller für den Frieden (Courage to Fear: Authors for Peace)* Collection Luchterhand, 415. Darmstadt 1982.

in 1939. Christian Democratic Union[1] defense expert Manfred Wörner[2] suggested in December 1979 that NATO needed to redefine its constitution. Its purpose, coming to the defense of a NATO country under attack, was no longer sufficient; genuine defense calls for preventive first strike. True defense is offensive! Defense is attack. He was repudiated by the Social Democratic Party[3] but to all intents and purposes the government concurred with his point of view. The stationing of 572 medium-range missiles in Western Europe is not "defense" by any stretch of the imagination. Neither is Jimmy Carter's Presidential Directive 59 of August 1980, which asserted that as far as the United States is concerned, a war fought with nuclear weapons was thinkable and conductible. What is new in this military policy is that it wipes out the old nebulous distinction between weapons which were to be used "only politically" as a threat and those which were intended for military use in an emergency. Atomic weapons were initially introduced as a mere political club; evidently that smoke screen is no longer regarded as necessary.

If the West were concerned simply with a credible deterrent, our second-strike capability would be sufficient. The point of the new arms race, however, is our attempt to achieve "first-strike capability" to enable us to carry out a disabling surprise attack. The 572 medium-range missiles intended for Western Europe provide this first-strike capability. We need only four minutes to turn the European portion of the Soviet Union into a field of rubble and corpses. Military propaganda does not, of course, speak of preparing an aggressive war; it talks about "advancing to defend" instead of attack; "preventive strike" for surprise attack; and "defense" has increasingly

1. Christian Democratic Union—a branch of the party that was then in opposition and came to lead the government in the latter part of 1982.

2. Then defense expert; became minister of defense under the Christian Democratic Party government of Chancellor Helmut Kohl.

3. The party then in power in Germany.

become the euphemism for war. For the Russians, this new threat is analogous to the United States being threatened by atomic missiles based in Cuba. What would the Americans do in such a situation with the least increase in tension? They would finish off Cuba, just in case. In exactly such a situation the Eastern powers would feel impelled to finish off Western Europe; that means that we here have become the first atomic target. Thus the arms buildup does not make us more secure; on the contrary, it endangers us far more than the threatening Russians.

The preparation of aggressive war is a crime under the law of nations and according to the constitutional law of the Federal Republic of Germany. Given this situation, *a new European peace movement* has arisen which seeks "too much" pacifism, according to some comments from Bonn. Is it possible to seek "too much" peace? The common denominator of all the people in this movement, which has support in churches, political parties, labor unions, and in the military, is more properly characterized as "nuclear pacifism," the rejection of the means of mass annihilation which are quite inappropriately referred to by the old-fashioned name of "weapons." After all, the purpose is not to destroy or to disable combatants, soldiers, fighters. Atomic weapons are tools of mass destruction turned against everything that lives. Nuclear pacifists are people who reject life under the protection of such instruments of mass murder, who do not want to defend themselves by means of atomic holocaust; who do not want to win an atomic war and who reject atomic blackmail. It is not by chance that the word "holocaust" has cropped up along the way: Hitler's gas, for example, the Zyclon B used at Auschwitz, cannot simply be declared a "weapon." Nuclear pacifism is the movement's unifying factor and what brings together its disparate groups such as radical, often Christian, pacifists, adherents of a "strategy of genuine defense" (Afheldt),[4] right up to conventional military strategists. This movement is new because it did not begin until after December 1979—at least not in Germany, in contrast to Holland; it is European because it pursues its own interests in opposition to the American government of the moment, and it is a broadly growing *movement*, cutting across political parties and the institutions of society. It is the self-expression of the masses and as such presents a new quality of democracy; the issue of atomic death or life is too important to be left to professional politicians.

Counterinformation to official government propaganda, countermedia, protests, and alternative thinking—all these are the expression of a new consciousness of people who no longer find themselves articulated by election machinery alone. Our fears are too deep to be sublimated into elections. Years ago, Willy Brandt[5] suggested that we should "dare a little more democracy" in West Germany. The peace movement cashes in on this promise by "daring a little more peace" than the government.

There are objections to this great democratic movement, which everyone active in it has already heard. The first and perhaps most dangerous objection is the charge of defeatism and resignation. It is phrased: "You'll never make it, in any case! Disarmament and peace would be well and good, but what will actually happen will be decided at the top. We are still totally dependent." This is based on partially valid insights such as: If new weapons systems are scientifically researched and militarily-technologically planned, then they will generally also be politically approved. Politics is largely an appendage of the functioning military-industrial complex. Beyond that, there is an economic interest in arms development that constitutes a secure investment opportunity. Be-

4. Horst Afheldt, advocate of "guerrilla stop," coined this phrase for a system of defense based on "techno-guerrillas."
5. Past chancellor of the German Federal Republic.

yond that, we are merely a satellite of the Americans; what could we possibly do? I regard such private and national feelings of impotence as being extremely dangerous. They are full of despair about democracy and about the people's right to self-determination. We have a lot to learn from smaller and even more dependent countries in Europe. I am thinking, for instance, of the Scandinavian peace women—five hundred thousand women who have organized. We women in Germany in particular have not the least reason to continue to see ourselves as objects of military policy. If you are not part of the solution, you are part of the problem.[6]

I remember a few incidents during the older peace movement of the 1950s. Often we were miserably small groups, including many older women in shabby coats. I missed the fellow students of my own age whom I would have preferred. Once Martin Niemöller addressed us. We were squeezed into the tiny seats of an elementary school classroom in Cologne-Ehrenfeld. I had attempted to interest a young, energetic journalist in that occasion. "That's not really worthwhile, just a bunch of little old peace ladies," was his response. I shall never forget this insult: a put-down of older people who had, after all, lived through two world wars, of women whom you don't have to take seriously, and of peace.

I want to tell you what I have learned from such bitter and demeaning experiences: a measure of inner independence. There are issues for which you must go into the streets, and speak a clear "no" in your workplace or in the union. If they tell you it will not do any good, and has no chance whatever, you must do it anyway, if only for the sake of your own human dignity, if only to be able to look your own children in the eye. If you keep silent today and allow yourself to be used, you are already dead. You have armed yourself to death!

6. Concerning the quotation in German, *Wer sich nicht wehrt, lebt verkehrt*, see n. 6, p. 46.

In the face of such feelings of impotence and defeatism, you must know exactly why you are doing all this and why it is essential for you, so that you do not cave in if they threaten you and intimidate you with censorship and blacklist you in your profession. We do not want to define our life as do those who are arming us to death.

The second objection that I hear runs: "You are so naive, you pacifists, such wide-eyed innocents. You do not really know what you are talking about, especially not the women." This objection is to the point, in as much as we need to become better informed. That is not so hard; don't be intimidated, even though you do have to overcome government propaganda. For more than thirty years now the arms race has been kept going by the technologically superior Americans inventing a "deterrence gap" whenever they want to introduce a new weapons system. Then the Russians follow right along.

What is the real scoop about the balance of deterrence? NATO and our government tell us: "If you speak out against Pershing, you have to speak out against SS–20," intending thus to prove the Soviet head start and superiority. But all this never includes all the atomic weapons in and for Europe— General Bastian,[7] in his elegant way, calls this deception in the calculation "grossly misleading."

I would prefer to call it the lie about our jeopardy in the interest of the arms race. Bastian bases his claim on neutral peace researchers who have demonstrated clearly that the West was superior and not inferior in the area of medium-range missiles without any further "catch-up effort." It is not the peace movement that is "naive" but the arms buildup promoters who stubbornly ignore neutral and critical peace research. We want to resist this intimidation by men, this

7. West Germany's retired General Gert Bastian is one of eleven former NATO generals who have appealed against the placement of Pershing II and Cruise missiles in Europe.

"you don't understand any of this." We understand the game very well, we know exactly *for whom* there are more important matters than peace, *which* nation wants to be number one, *whence* the neutron devices may be effectively launched, *just what* a so-called limited nuclear war will be limited to, *who* believes they may carry out and win such a war.

The third charge that we hear is that we are so one-sided. Perhaps none of these charges is as accurate as this one. Indeed, we are one-sidedly for life and against the threat of nuclear holocaust. One of the most one-sided slogans hails from Holland. "Liberate the world from nuclear weapons and begin in the Netherlands!" Why not begin in the Federal Republic of Germany? To continue hoping for negotiations does not suffice. We must surely risk a little more peace than arms control talks. The ratification of SALT I pushed arms limits upward in certain ways; the disarmament treaty positively invited a new round of arms development. Further, the so-called negotiations functioned like bad legislation. Crime evades, the criminals circumvent the law. The scientists and technicians, the arms planners and weapons profiteers, military leaders and strategists utilize the limitation of one method of overkill as a challenge to invent new, superior means. Even if the negotiations were carried on at the level of experts, they would not change much. They have been negotiating for more than thirty years! You can see what that has produced.

That is why the peace movement cannot be appeased by the government's repeated assurances to stand by the so-called double-track decision. The term "double track" is all but unknown in the American discussion. Everyone there knows that the issue is arms buildup without any "ifs" and "buts." Even if the United States government makes some concessions for its German friends, it is increasingly clear that it has no intention of negotiating the positioning of Pershing II missiles, as stated by Eugene Rostow, former head of the U.S.

Disarmament Agency. It is therefore not clear whether any negotiations are seriously intended, which weapons systems are still subject to negotiations, and whether these improbable negotiations could ever lead to more than setting upper numerical limits. I doubt that these negotiations can effect peace. When I began to concern myself seriously with peace research a year and a half ago, I still believed in arms control negotiations—SALT II, etc. I thought bilaterally then. In the meantime, together with the majority of the European peace movement, I have moved to a unilateral position. We advocate one-sided (unilateral) disarmament, to be taken step by step, gradually.

This is backed by the following considerations: the only way to change anything is to begin with yourself. All historical experience of the past thirty years contradicts the hope of achieving a limitation of this madness through bilateral negotiations. There is negotiation and nothing changes. That is the bitter truth. We must therefore make it clear that we renounce protection by further atomic weapons, that we seek a nuclear-weapon-free zone for Europe, whether this suits the superpowers or not. Such a new and European politics will prove immensely attractive to all the peoples of Europe, including those behind the Iron Curtain. The Federal Republic can play an important role in this. It is obvious that such a peace movement, carried by grass roots support, cannot come from the East and cannot unfold there.

What good is our democracy and our few additional basic rights and basic freedoms, if we do not use them to risk a little more peace?

The difference between East and West is not found in what military experts here and there have to say about nuclear warheads. If there is a difference, then it must be seen in us, in a public stand for unilateral disarmament by the peace movement.

I am a unilateralist. That means: I do not believe that the

madness becomes rational simply because both sides carry it out in an orderly and agreed-upon manner. Some groups in our country sign two-sided, bilateral appeals to the governments in East and West. Please do stop, at last, they say. Often it sounds like worried mothers calling out. In reality this bilateralism is politically and morally impotent. We deceive ourselves into the position of a spectator: the mother facing rambunctious boys. But in truth we are deeply involved, we pay for the madness, we tolerate it, we elect the officials of the lunatic asylum to which we are assigned. We, the innocent tax-paying citizens, are part of the murderous system. If we truly want peace, we must begin where we are, on this our side, necessarily one-sidedly.

It is rationalistic stupidity to assume that the mutual threat of murder could be removed from this world as a kind of business transaction. Both sides give a little and at once we have beautiful balance! The conflict is too serious for such illusions. The truth is that one side must begin, one of us must drop the threats, one of us must take a tiny step forward, *alone*. Those who think bilaterally are condemned to impotence; they will never break the circle. Who is in a position to take the step forward, unilaterally, toward peace?

During a Washington prayer service for peace they sang an old spiritual. "It's me, it's me, standing in the need of prayer. It's me, oh Lord, standing in the need of prayer. Not my brother, not my sister, it's me, oh Lord . . ." Various verses of this hymn were adapted to the theme of this worship service. "Not the Russians, not the Cubans, not the Persians, . . . it's me, oh Lord, standing in the need of prayer." To work in the peace movement and to stand up for peace means to grasp this existential moment: it's me, oh Lord. There is a religious root to the peace movement even among those who see themselves as postreligious. People know that this matter of peace involves them absolutely; it is the "ultimate concern," as Paul Tillich said to paraphrase the word "God." This issue which concerns me absolutely, without which I cannot live, depends on my decision and my actions. I cannot carry it forward as a bilateral spectator. I am responsible for *my* government, for my country, and its medium-range missiles. I live here on this side of the border. Peace is an existential issue because it is a theological one. I need peace. Possibly Mr. Brezhnev does not find it quite so necessary—or perhaps he needs it even more, as many cynics in Washington believe. But that does not speak to our need and to our dilemma.

God, too, acted in a mighty unilateral manner when he began to live unarmed and vulnerable, that is, as a human being.

10

WHEN LIFE FREEZES OVER*

"If we say we have no sin, we deceive ourselves, and the truth is not in us."

1 John 1:8

When I attempt to explain how I experience our world, I cannot shake an image that imposes itself upon me and holds me prisoner: the glacier—that slow advance of frigidity, this process of frost which we experience and try to forget. A glacial period in schools, on the assembly line, in high-rise apartments, in those mini-units that used to be called "family." We all know that there is ever more and more sophisticated torture, that there is more hunger than ever before, that in the Third World more children are intellectually handicapped for lack of protein. At the same time, more and more people are spiritually handicapped because of "overnutrition," to coin a phrase for the condition we enjoy. Not only do we live in an advancing glacial period, we produce it, we maintain it, and profit from it. To deny this "sin," the dominion of the frost line over the retreating people would be absurd. You have to be enormously insensitive or dense to deny or to ignore the above New Testament quotation. You don't have to be "religious" or "overly sensitive" or "a typical woman" to understand what I am talking about. Sin, the absence of warmth, love, compassion, trust, is the most normal condition.

Marianne is a pretty young woman who lives with her

*First published in the original German text of this book.

children in her suburban home. She tells me about the gold jewelry that her husband gave her at Christmas. The gold comes from South Africa, but she does not know that there is blood on her chain; she hardly understands the connection between racism, infant mortality, and exploitation on the one hand and profit, a favorable rate for gold, and the export of nuclear technology, in which her husband is involved, on the other hand. She also does not (yet) know that gold does not keep you warm. "Sin" is a ridiculously old-fashioned word for her—she relates it to eating too much whipped cream, illegal parking, and sexual behavior. None of this is to be taken seriously. Marianne feels guilty about her mother because she does not spend enough time with her; occasionally she will question whether she brings her children up correctly in every way. But sin? Lately she has frequently been depressed without being able to identify the reason. Soon, I suspect, the emptiness of her life will catch up with her. Then she will either have to change her life, or she will continue in her modernized doll's house and continue to deny, to suppress, to sweep under the ever-thicker carpet whatever is disturbing or challenging. She will continue to freeze up, despite high intelligence, a normal education sufficient for civilized conversation, and a native capacity to empathize with suffering and joy. She will remain underdeveloped rationally and emotionally, socially, and therefore also individually—a colonized being, governed by trends that she does not help set but to which she submits; cut off from life, depoliticized and impoverished as a matter of course.

Marianne does not know this. Were she to read these lines, she would regard them as vast and overly pessimistic exaggerations. Like most people, she is superficially Christianized. Once upon a time she heard that sin means separation from God, turning away from the Creator, rebelliousness toward him, worship of other gods. But all these are empty formulas which have nothing to do with her life. She most nearly understands being separated from God, the situation described by the word "sin," during her depressions. Being more sensitive to cold than her husband, she senses the approaching ice age. But there are so many fantastic anti-depressants; alcohol is the most widespread answer to the experience of sin in our culture.

When our tradition tells us that sin is the destruction of our relationship with God, it does not concern itself with particular "sins" but with the total condition, that is, the destruction of our capacity to relate. Everything becomes shadowy, unimportant; it no longer tastes good; you can take it or you can leave it. Sin means being separated from the foundation of life, disturbed in our relation to

—ourselves
—our neighbors
—creation
—the human family.

Marianne regards herself as a victim of circumstances. Thanks to feminine education, she does not know her own strength and abilities. It has long since been washed into her brain that she cannot fix electric wiring, that only young and pretty women may speak on television, that of course economics and politics are beyond her. When I asked her recently to sign the appeal of Danish women against the so-called "catching-up arms buildup," she came up with the classic argument: "That does not do any good anyway." For women more so than for others, sin means not to know yourself, your own strength and abilities, never to have experienced solidarity and therefore not to know anything about its power, not to expect anything from yourself. It means living without self-determination, without strength or power, without hope. Black theologians in South Africa describe as powerlessness the apathy of those who have given up on themselves. The life of most

women is similar to that of the colonized. Alcoholism is thus
an almost "natural" consequence of the destruction of one's
ability to relate to oneself.

Marianne's relationship to her neighbor is, to put it kindly,
rather limited. She only socializes with people of her own
class. She protects her children from any contact with other
people, other experiences, any other culture—unconsciously,
you understand. Please no Turks[1] in our neighborhood or
school or sports club. The racism that she lives is unques-
tioned. But even relations with people of her own class are
built essentially on competition and envy. What they can
afford! (Instead of: Whatever do they need that for?) Why do
your friends do better at school? (Instead of: What are you
really interested in just now?) How come your colleague got
his promotion first? (Instead of: How can we find more time
for each other?) The assumption that the other man, the other
woman, is one's enemy instead of one's richness, one's confir-
mation, one's joy is the constant foundation of the culture in
which we live, plastered over by pleasant parties.

Marianne's bonds with creation and nature are perhaps a
little less disrupted than her husband's. She bicycles, he
drives. But she has lost her original pleasure in the returning
birds, the rising moon. Everything that she loved as a very
young girl is now more remote, a matter of indifference. But
she is still fighting the glacial process.

Marianne's bond with the human family, for example, with
sisters from the Third World, is in disarray, privatistic, crip-
pled. I have given up answering her occasional query: "But
what could we possibly do?" This sweet, innocent girl's question simply covers up that she has no real intention of doing
anything. There are hundreds of opportunities to be rele-
vantly and efficiently engaged and to devote a portion of your

---

1. The currently largest group of "temporary" foreign laborers ("guest
workers") in Germany.

time, your money, your energy to justice. Did people really ask as naively in 1943, when mass deportations of Jews were rolling through Germany?

In a letter from an Indonesian father I read the following:

> Every father seeks to better life for his children. That is why he became a father. My daughter became a prostitute. It was the only way she could help the family. She does not want to watch as the family starves to death. A victim of poverty, my God. I feel ashamed. But the wealthy society can only buy our bodies, not our souls.
>
> My wife is a very symbol of womanhood, full of suffering and innumerable sacrifices, my God. She works as a maid for 1,200 rupees [about $2.00] a month and one meal a day. She has to do all the heavy household work: laundry, cleaning, cooking, looking after the master's children, and all that for these lousy 1,200 rupees. The master's wife does not notice my wife's labor. My children, too, could use some concern and love, but circumstances force my own wife to neglect her own household, in order to take care of other people's—for such a pittance. Can community grow in such desolation?
>
> How can a man with brains allow his wife to be a slave and his daughter a prostitute; children of hunger—naked, sick, uneducated?[2]

Word has spread that sin has precious little to do with masturbation. Does this letter have something to do with sin, with our entirely personal guilt? To become an adult means to become capable of guilt and shame.

My understanding of sin is stamped by the experiences of my generation (born 1929). I am a child of fascism. I spent about ten years of my young adulthood with the questions "How could it happen? Where were you when they corralled those transports? Did you smell nothing of the gas?" Without this background, I would probably still think about sin in terms of the superficial nonsense taught by a miserable religious socialization. To be an adult means to be able to know

2. *Publik Forum*, a Frankfurt bi-weekly, 14 December 1979.

guilt. To understand what sin is, you need a measuring tape with which to measure false, unconscious, frozen life. Sin can be recognized and overcome only when we begin to use this measure, when we begin to love one another. A voice calls: Turn and live! Why will you die? (Ezek. 18:31).

11

THE NEW QUEST FOR GOD*

Recently I wrote an article for an explicitly left-wing journal. I closed with a couple of sentences about God, and I was not sure whether I could inflict this on the editors and readers of that journal. The editor called, thanked me for the article: very good, only a bit too long. I said that perhaps you could cut the ending; it is perhaps too pious for you. Oh no, came the response from the other end of the line. That says something to me, said the young editor, indeed, a great deal. And I think many other readers will have the same reaction. So we left the two sentences about God in the manuscript, and I asked myself, what has changed in these past years?

In the autumn of 1981 the author Martin Walser[1] was awarded the Georg-Büchner Prize of the Academy for Linguistics and Literature in Darmstadt.[2] There he gave a speech with the title "What Makes God Die?" Walser described Büchner's novella *Lenz* ("Spring") as the "struggle of the traumatized against trauma. He is in need of God." Walser

*Broadcast over Germany's Southwest Radio in Baden-Baden, 1 November 1981, in the series *Blick in die Zeit* ("Looking at Our Age"). First reprinted in the *Evangeliche Kommentare* ("Protestant Commentaries") 2, 1982.

1. German writer (b.1927). Several of his works are available in English, including *Beyond All Love* and *A Runaway Horse*.
2. The prize, one of the prestigious German literary prizes, honors the life and work of Georg Büchner (1813–37). Best known for the dramas *Dantos Tod* ("Danton's Death"), *Leonce and Lena*, and the fragment *Woczeck*. He had to flee his native Hesse after publishing a revolutionary pamphlet *Der hessiche Landbote* ("The Hessian Country Messenger").

mentioned that we have canonized a literature without demands. "May we not gain the impression that more and more literature specializes in less and less?" Walser objects to the undemanding nature of characters who glorify their own hopelessness, to their absolute invectives, and he finds an ally in Büchner's atheism grown out of pain.

I want to give you a third anecdote about God's appearance in an unexpected locale. Angi Domdey, the singer of the group "Snow White," speaks at the end of one of her songs of the power in us and about God. Some women from the radical women's movement were outraged and asked that the reference be deleted. But it stayed, as the young editor told me, because it says so much to so many.

These are three anecdotes about God in places where it has not been usual to speak about God. They are reports from a post-Christian world. The people with whom they originate have nothing to do with organized religion. Often they and their friends have left the churches. They would surely not call themselves Christians. For years, religion for many of them has been something dead. Absolutely trivial. For pollsters with questions such as "Do you believe in God?" they presumably have the ready standard response "I am not religious." Just as someone might say: I am not much into sports. Or: I have no ear for music. Or: Egyptology is not my field. Friendly, polite distance toward an outdated concern. I hesitate to call these people non-Christians or unbelievers, for such terms presuppose a conscious decision which for the majority of people is not even a matter for discussion. They are simply post-Christians, living in an age where the question of faith and unbelief was not ever and could never become their question.

When I as a Christian used to be together with such post-Christians, I always had the feeling that I must apologize, that I should explain why a normally intelligent person "still," as they said, holds fast to God.

But that is precisely what has changed. It is now easier for me to open up, I am less ashamed, and I can explain what my love of God has to do with my despair over the culture in which we live.

With due caution, I would like to affirm that I regard these three reports from the cultural scene as significant: signs of change, of a new attention, a break with the culture for which God was about as important as Egyptology. I still assert this haltingly and with some embarrassment, because I do not believe that this new quest for God will once again fill the churches, because I would not like to see this questing after God become involved with the "in God we trust" on the American dollar or with the "God with us" on the belt buckles of the old German army. Quite other needs and longings, uncertainties and fears, play a role in this new inquiry. Schoolchildren of the post-Christian culture, who have therefore also grown up more or less free of religion, sometimes pose the questions like this: What does Christianity really mean? What good did it do? Why were people attached to it? Did they actually lead different lives if they were Christians? Did they know the meaning of life? In what way is a Christian different from a non-Christian?

This question: Does God make a difference? can only become visible when the matter-of-course acceptance of Christianity has passed away; when the church no longer stands in the center of the village, because the village is no longer the people's universe; when we have moved away from the unity of homeland, village, and religion. This question about God comes newly and impatiently precisely from post-Christian urbanites. They miss something in their life—a steadiness, a consolation, a certainty, a guideline, a meaning. They cannot and will not be satisfied with life as it simply happens to be. They have grasped the wanton undemandingness implied by the post-Christian pose, the "I am not religious." As Walser sees it, it is an attempt to achieve authenticity by regression. I would call it a way of being dead, that is, without hope, without vision, and therefore without involvement and without relevance.

One day recently, a student attending my lecture said something quite honest in front of 330 people. Something like: "Actually, I really feel quite comfortable. I have no questions. At the same time I am dissatisfied because I have no questions. You have just spoken about spiritual hunger; that scared me. I should love to be hungry, but I am not."

The trouble with hungering after God is that, even though it returns again and again, just like physical hunger, it is easily diverted and reprogrammed. Then you forget it, fill your guts with other things and declare "I am not religious." This trivial phrase strikes me roughly as if someone were saying: "I don't really care that my sister is being raped and my brother is dying in a psychiatric hospital; I am blind in both eyes anyway, and I don't know what it means to dance; I am just not religious."

We need God out of anguish, fear, and rage; those are the outcast sisters and brothers of love. If we once again allow ourselves to be touched by pain, fear, and rage, then we can escape this undemandingness that we ask no more of life than our daily sandwich.

There was a time when God was part of the daily bread. God-talk was universal, understandable by all. That kind of speaking preserved the vision of life in which everyone had enough to eat. Today we lack that vision, and food has become a private matter. But human beings are not that undemanding, that barren of vision, that mindless, that turned on to money and career. For the hunger for God is not something that can be extirpated. That is the reason we have a peace movement in our land.

12

NEVER AGAIN
HIROSHIMA*

I shall speak to the topic "Paul Tibbetts, Euroshima, and Resistance," but I want to propose a rule for what I want to say. I also wish that it be applied to what you hear: namely, that the victims of Hiroshima and Nagasaki, the dead and the *hibakusha*, the survivors of a nuclear attack, be present in our remembrance. I mean this strictly, as a writer who treats words with precision. I do not wish to speak any words that cannot stand up before the dead and the survivors. And I do not want to leave out any words that the dead and the survivors might have a right to expect. The victims are here with us. They are a part of the vast realm of the living and the dead. And should we see only the light side of this total world, only the living, then we exile ourselves from this kingdom and destroy ourselves.

Paul Tibbetts, the pilot of the Hiroshima atomic bomber, was asked during an interview with IG Metall[1] whether he has a bad conscience on August 6, when the victims of Hiroshima are remembered throughout the world. He stated the following: "No, I do not bother with that. I don't think about it. All that is past. Hiroshima is history. It was a lesson to teach us certain things. But there are too many new and interesting developments in my life. I need to think about these every day, much more than about something like Hiroshima. I do not live in the past."

*Speech given on 15 November 1981 at the opening of an exhibition of documents, "Hiroshima-Nagasaki," in Hamburg.
1. The German metalworkers' union.

The transcript of this interview should be included in every reader for schoolchildren. It would also be good to use it in the military's officer training courses. Is Paul Tibbetts a clean-cut, clear-speaking, almost certainly incorruptible, and therefore "decent" officer, a model? I can draw three themes from the interview that he granted which are likely to be important for the training of officers today: playing down—obedience—forgetting.

Playing down: "It really was not all that many. Far more people died elsewhere. What we bombarded were military targets. Everybody else would have done the same: Germans, Russians."

Obedience: "I did not have any authority to decide. It was not up to me to make a decision. I grew up as a soldier. I have been trained to follow orders by competent authority."

Forgetting: "I do not bother with that. I have no regrets."

The Paul Tibbetts interview is illustrated by a photograph. You see the broad-shouldered Tibbetts smiling into the camera, slightly gray and with eyeglasses, but still the same old reliable, dashing pilot. His hand is stretched out from his body as if it were no longer part of him. He has left it with another person in the picture, a Japanese nun, a Hiroshima survivor with keloids,[2] that is, with the scarlet scar tissue growth which can develop in the healing of atomic burns.

Paul Tibbetts, who has no regrets, has given his hand to the *hibakusha*. He is grinning, she is serious. The camera is focused on him; she stands back. He is a man, and an officer. She is only a woman, half a person. He was the pilot, the culprit, she was on the ground, a victim. This photograph is an unbearable insult: it is racist, sexist, militarist, and imperialist. The handshake between these two is supposed to show

2. Keloids, excessive growth in scar tissue, rare in Caucasians but common for various kinds of scars among people of color. They developed on many of the victims of atomic burns.

reconciliation. Before I saw this photo, I had not known that a lie can be photographed so clearly and quite without shame.

Play down—obey—forget . . . once you have learned that then you can also bare your upper incisors in order to produce a grimace that may perhaps have once meant a smile. Let us ask ourselves just how far *we* are being trained in precisely such activities, precisely where we appropriate what is required if you want to smile successfully: the playing down, obeying, forgetting. What does our government demand from our people if it is not playing down (no scare campaign, it is a military necessity!)—obeying (the experts know better!)—forgetting (let us not talk so much about fascism, the situation is really quite different today!). How far do we go along with it: playing down—obeying—forgetting?

Since 1980 there has been a new word in our language, Euroshima. When I first heard it, I was shocked: can you do this to the victims of Hiroshima—cut their name in half, take away their death, and generalize it? But the more I think about it, the more appropriate I find this new European word, this call: no Euroshima. It revives memories. It makes Americans aware of their anti-Japanese racism. After all, Europe is not Asia. If you ask yourself why the Americans dropped the atomic bomb on a defeated people at the last minute, there are two possible answers, neither of which has anything to do with Japan and the Japanese people, just as Paul Tibbetts has no connection with the Japanese woman. One answer is: it was a scientific experiment. The cities of Hiroshima and Nagasaki had deliberately not been bombed earlier with conventional weapons in order to establish exactly what kind of damage is caused by an atomic bomb. The macabre fact that a special American hospital was set up to examine but not to treat the victims, regarding them as guinea pigs but not as victims, speaks for this interpretation: a new experiment.

The second motive advanced for dropping the atomic bomb is that the bomb carried an unmistakable message for the

Soviet Union, documenting the military strength and superiority of the United States.

Both the scientific and the anticommunist arguments come up in the current debate. We all live under the rule of the MIC, the military-industrial complex.[3] It is not enemy superiority that forces us to develop new bombs, to test poison gases, and make them operational. Rather, the MIC thrives on the production of death and defines scientific progress as progress in overkill. In this connection, Euroshima has yet another meaning. The bombs that hit the victims then, hit us also. It is not as if what happens to one member of the human family were not significant for the others. It is not true that we can live with the bomb because we are preparing it only for others.

"The shock paralyzed the survivors. For days and weeks they sat apathetically in the ruins, unable to understand what had happened, what they had experienced. Many people fled the burning cities in a trance. They were horrified by the appearance of the other victims of the atom bomb without realizing that they themselves were disfigured and burnt all over their bodies."

I am trying to read this eyewitness report of a survivor as its truth applies to us. Do not we here in Euroshima live in a trance, unable to understand what is happening to us? We have to discard the notion that the arms race is preparedness, is a potential warning, is intended for later and, we hope, for never. That is a lie. You cannot pay taxes for the nuclear holocaust, train its intelligence, carry on research, deal with its impact on health by legislation, teach children about military science, prepare women for their future role in the army, and carry on all the preparatory activity as a mere precaution, as if it were not meant seriously. Everything we do today with

3. President Dwight D. Eisenhower is generally credited with coining this term in his farewell radio and television address to the American people, 17 January 1961.

our money, our intellect, our energy, our culture, all the
activities I would summarize as militarization of the society:
industrial militarization; political militarization; psychological
militarization; economic militarization—all this does not spell
preparedness. It shows us possessed by a death wish and the
urge to kill. This is the barrage of propaganda under which we
live nowadays. One example of this occurs when the speech
commemorating the war dead on Memorial Day can be given
by the Secretary of Defense, he who every day deals with the
megadead who are planned into his scenarios. The threshold
of safety beyond which we may kill is to be lowered—an
atomic warning shot, a strictly limited atomic war—we are to
get used to that so that Paul Tibbetts's mechanism will also be
triggered in us. Play down—obey—forget! But we still flee
from the images that surround us here.

In 1945 General Douglas MacArthur, the American com-
mander-in-chief, forbade Japanese doctors and scientists from
publishing their insights into atomic sickness in any shape or
manner. Films, photographs, and other documents were
banned, eyewitness reports were suppressed. How about us?
Can we see, hear, touch? We live and obey and carry on in a
state of apathy, of anesthesia, as if life had not changed in our
ever more self-militarized country, as if the bomb could not
touch us because it is meant only for others, only for later,
only for a real emergency.

No, it is here, it is inside of us and has anesthetized us. It
rules over us. The bombs are falling now, as the American
peace movement puts it. For me this has a double meaning:
the bombs are falling on the poorest of the poor. Every minute
a child under two years of age dies of starvation. Another one
is dying as I speak this sentence. The bombs are falling now
on those we allow to die of hunger and other curable diseases.
We continue the massacre of people who have done nothing
but come into this world with the wrong skin color in the
wrong country. Our militarists, we all know, are faced with

other worries and other problems. But we should not allow ourselves to be anesthetized to the point where we cannot clearly recognize the connection.

The bombs are also falling on us. The death machine which we service, for which we think, carry on politics, go vote, invest, and train, this MIC machine in which we are but a cog, determines our life. That is what is killing us! The arms race kills, even without war! Those who still think, who still feel, feel insecure in the security state. The preparation of an aggressive nuclear war is a crime under the law of nations and under the basic law of the Federal Republic of Germany.

The stationing of 572 medium-range missiles, each one with forty times the power of a little Hiroshima bomb, constitutes that crime. There is no region in the world where more people are crammed in together with as many bombs, missiles, and nuclear power stations as in the Federal Republic of Germany. We sit on that powder keg, we live with this cancer. What is our answer? What will you do when you have seen these pictures and gone home? Play it down—obey—forget—that is the lesson of pilot Paul Tibbetts. If you think and act that way, you are possessed by the bomb.

It is time to resist. The American President Truman said in 1948 that the atomic bomb saved the lives of two hundred and fifty thousand Allied soldiers and as many Japanese. He concludes this megadeath arithmetic with the remark: "I think the sacrifice of Hiroshima and Nagasaki was necessary for the future of both Japan and the Allied nations." We think differently. Their sacrifice was not necessary, it was a crime. If the death of Hiroshima is to have any meaning, it is to teach and to warn us. Then the dead become meaningful to the Japanese peace movement—and Japan is to be forced into the same American madness as we (*m*utually *a*ssured *d*estruction)— then the dead have meaning for the growing North American peace movement and then they are meaningful to us. The world is made up of the dead and the living, and to become human we must listen to the voice of the dead. One Hiroshima and one Nagasaki was enough.

13

HOPE UNTO
THE YEAR 2000?*

If you ask me about the year 2000—but I am a woman, so you had better not ask me at all—but if you ask me: I am afraid. My stomach ties into knots when I think of the year 2000, I lose my appetite, my mouth dries up, I cannot breathe properly. Talk about breath: shall we still breathe without air filters and gas masks in the year 2000?

I am European and during the last several years I have spent part of my time in the United States. Surely, there are still considerable differences between Hamburg-Altona and Manhattan, but to me they are becoming less and less significant: it is the so-called "First World" in which I live; they are both countries which according to the Trilateral Commission belong in the first category, top level as far as standard of living and consumption of energy are concerned.

In practice that means: among my acquaintances death is due to overindulgence, not hunger. To neuroses, not ignorance. To fear, not riots. To lack of faith, not to superstition. I belong to the middle middle class, privileged through education, set apart by "the little difference,"[1] endangered by the internal repression which has so changed the climate in our country, increasingly intimidating and isolating so many intellectuals.

I mention all this so that you will better understand why I

*Broadcast over Bavarian radio, 1980.
1. *Der kleine Unterschied,* "the difference between men and women," an expression popularized in Germany by Alice Schwarzer, through her book, *Emma: Der kleine Unterschied.*

am fearful of the year 2000. Not because I am special but because I have been injured precisely as have most of my generation, who will be about seventy years old in the year 2000. I am a child of fascism, raised during the nights of the air raids, grown up in the period of remilitarization, and if you ask me about the year 2000 that is what comes immediately to mind: a basic feeling of fear.

Let me try to spell out my fears: a shopping list of terror— that is the most I can do in the face of this date, two thousand years after the birth of Christ—but no glass menagerie this, God knows. Based on what is, what I perceive, I've tried to imagine what shall be.

My cues are: militarization and state terror; macrotechnology and more people starving to death; an ice age of human relations.

While I write this radio talk, the arms race is being escalated to a new level in Bonn and Brussels. Medium-range missiles are to become Euro-missiles. They are being introduced so that we may then be able to negotiate. In order to reduce arms we must first build up arms. New words are being invented as a smoke screen to hide the massive arms buildup that they describe: we call it "catching up" or "modernization," but the strategy of the hawks in Bonn and Washington is the same: first an arms buildup, then negotiations. Only an occasional voice advocates the reverse sequence: negotiate first and then, perhaps under new conditions, arm.

What will the arms spiral look like in twenty years? No one who advocates preventive arms buildup today can seriously believe in being able to turn back the spiral later, through negotiations.

I do not know whether in military history there has ever been a situation where it was possible to take back the toy once a planning general staff, a military organization, let alone an economic lobby, has the dynamite deal safely in their pocket. The switches were thrown in December 1979. The train could derail, or be brought to a halt by catastrophe, but it cannot take a direction other than that planned by those in authority.

I am afraid of the growing acquiescence with which we watch and accept that tanks damage our roads, firing ranges take over our resort areas, barracks educate our young people, and the burden of military expenditure undermines our educational and social services.

Some little while ago the defense lobby initiated a discussion on when women might finally enter the *Bundeswehr*.[2] From the start the question was not whether, but when. And that is quite consistent: military technological escalation calls for psychological preparation. Brains have to be washed. Expectations are raised, such as training opportunities for young girls with a technological interest for whom there are no positions in our economy. A certain readiness for military service is created by means of discussion groups—quite balanced in presenting both the pros and the cons, of course.

The existing world status quo needs to be protected militarily: the international division of labor between us, the exporters from the macro-technologies, and the zones of lowest salaries and cheapest labor force. The pauperization of these countries where it does not pay to invest, especially if they have no dictators, in contrast to South Africa, Brazil, or Gabon, is part of the scheme. Our structure of injustice demands defense; the apartheid which we support technologically and commercially requires security. More than ever before, property and militarization, markets and armaments are closely linked.

It is more than eight hundred years since Francis of Assisi, asked whether his life without possessions was not hard and excessively burdensome, answered: "If we were to own things, then we would need weapons to defend ourselves.

2. The current West German army.

That is precisely what causes all the strife and battle and blocks love. That is the reason we do not wish to own anything."

As far as the military budget is concerned, about a third of a fifty-nine billion West German mark budget goes into the defense coffers. A society that will do that may rightfully be called "militarized." A country with the strongest European military and police force will appear as militarist at least in the eyes of its neighbors.

The feeling of living in an occupied country that currently afflicts the most sensitive will perhaps affect most people by the year 2000. Police identity checks: never be without your ID card! Questioning that becomes interrogation, intimidation, "bugging"—these are among the first political experiences today among young people in the ecological movement. What are you doing here? Can you identify yourself? It's not the police officer who is asked these questions, but the ordinary citizen, the bicyclist, grandma, and all others who are still strolling about without gas mask, ID card, or uniform.

The atomic energy program can be carried out only if parts of the private economic sector are put under special or military jurisdiction. Special regulations, illegal controls, and surveillance apparatus are then the order of the day. The planned arms buildup necessitates nuclear technology, or, translated into the friendly language of the occupying forces: in order to modernize our military defense arsenal, we need nuclear power plants. We now have an energy surplus of fifty-six percent, even at peak periods. That would be more than adequate, if it were not for the arms race. No lights would flicker out.

I am afraid of the spiral: weapons systems—nuclear technology—erosion of democracy—more weapons systems. Democratic rights such as that of public discussion, or that of workers to strike, have to be suspended within the orbit of nuclear technology. The atomic state must fundamentally change the life of its inhabitants: people will have to come to terms with being under surveillance, informed, directed, and evacuated. Planning for catastrophe cannot be based on democratic citizens.

Ecological problems and the achievement of alternative energy sources will demand all our financial and intellectual resources in the coming decades. Every dollar and every brain which we devote to maintenance of our stone-age style of relationships with other nations is lost to the efforts to solve the central issues of humanity. It is already clear that we are more concerned with macrotechnology than with a small technology that is "user friendly." Centralization of the economy and of administration is more important than democratizing decision-making and dispersing it to middle and lower levels.

In the United States, half of every one hundred scientists work directly or indirectly for "defense."[3] Fifty percent work simply to improve overkill. For this combination of economic interests, scientific research, and military might, the Americans have coined the expression "military-industrial complex," or simply, "the system."[4] I would rather use a biblical term and call it "the beast." The great beast out of the depths with its seven heads: more energy, more progress, more overkill, more profit, more world market, more torture, more living standard. I fear that beast with the seven heads (Revelation 13).

In 1972, one could buy a barrel, that is, 59 liters, of oil in the Third World for 26 kilograms of bananas; today you have to pay two hundred kilograms of bananas for it. What will those who work the land be able to obtain for their products by the year 2000? All of the Third World is affected by their inclusion in the world market, forced upon them by the industrialized

3. Based on research by SIPRI—Stockholm International Peace Research Institute.

4. The term was first coined by President Dwight D. Eisenhower. See n. 3, p. 100.

countries, and the resultant destruction of their local, internal markets: the silent war of the rich against the poor.

In many fertile regions of the Americas where rice, corn, and beans used to be grown, you will now find the plantations of the multinational companies. What is grown are strawberries and flowers for export, while the population starves and children are mentally retarded for lack of protein, the old perish and young people leave the land. For whose benefit are the strawberries and flowers grown? Who profits? And who does not really care much?

I am scared of the year 2000. Such a system of injustice on a world scale must affect the psyche of every one of us. Already we have the highest rate of children's suicide in the German Federal Republic—five hundred a year. We have about eighty thousand drug-dependent youth. Forty percent of our students are under psychological care, or are looking for it. The psychic misery that surrounds us is a function of our economic, political, and spiritual situation: we export weapons and nuclear technology. But is profit the only return to us? Does the death that we export not hit back? Does exploitation make the exploiter happy?

We are the closest allies of South Africa's policy of apartheid. Not only that—we vote against the poor and for the rich in every world trade conference. Can anyone assume that this will not produce consequences for the people of our country? We discriminate against our best writers, "clean up" school books and television programs. Can anyone assume that this does not affect our intellectual climate? Foreign observers are surprised at the frigid relationships between people in the Federal Republic of Germany. Workers and employees are quite aware of how meaningless their work is; men and women suffer from the emptiness and interchangeability of their relationships; the children and adolescents rage aggressively and destructively against others and themselves—they are the domestic side of the foreign policy coin, the psychic consequences of a design for living which is indeed based on worship of the great beast.

Are there hopes for the year 2000 and for all of us? Perhaps it is Christianity that taught me to be afraid because it upholds such a rich, emphatic, such a beautiful understanding of a true life. As a Christian you always demand more than custom provides. That is why I cannot sit content with the apocalypse brought to us courtesy of the military-nuclear system. Submission kills. And if you think that you were born too late into too old a world which can no longer be changed, then you lack faith. There is resistance to nuclear holocaust, there are signs of hope in communal living, there are groups who are as prepared as Abraham was to leave the straitjacket of the system and to opt for life, regardless of the sacrifice.

The fact that the government of the Netherlands has rejected the stationing of medium-range missiles is such a sign of peace—the piece of the rainbow between God and a world that is no longer cursed. In the United States there are numbers of young people who are willling to share that scarce commodity, work, who will jointly take one job, lower their standard of living, and increase their freedom.

I collect signs of hope, alternative stories, reports of the healing of the blind. That is how I work on my fears and turn swords and armored halftracks into plowshares and schoolbuses for which we shall have much use unto the year 2000.